ENDORSEMENTS

My close friendship with Patsy Cameneti began in 1978 when she was a student at the then Rhema Bible Training Center. My many years-long prayer relationship with her was with a small group of 7 or so women who regularly met and spent days sequestered together in prayer. We called ourselves "The Sparkies." Why? Because during our days of Bible study and prayer, one would spark another. Such glorious times! Working together with God. One thing we studied in detail and prayed fervently about was what the Bible calls "the end of days." So yes! I know Patsy knew what she was writing about. And I know you will be increased in the knowledge of these things by what she wrote herein.

Dr. Billye Brim
Billye Brim Ministries
Branson, Missouri

My friend, Patsy Cameneti, was such a blessing to the body of Christ and a true champion for the Lord. Patsy's book, *Kingdom Strategies for End-Time Prophetic Prayer,* gives us some golden nuggets from her life's journey as a prayer warrior and watchman to our nation and the nations. We can glean from her life experiences of prayer and intimacy with the Father, knowing your authority and the power that has been given to us as His intercessors, as well as her teaching gift on prayer strategies for both individuals and praying in groups. Patsy's prophetic insight into times and seasons always aligned with God's Word. She speaks to you as an individual on the role of the Church and on kingdom mentality, knowing His grace and peace and her hunger and passion for God's Church to walk in her full potential. This book will encourage you to be a prayer warrior and become a prayer champion for Christ.

Reverend Margaret Court, AC MBE
Senior Pastor, Victory Life Centre Inc.
Perth, Australia

Patsy Cameneti was one of those rare voices who could take the deep things of God and make them immediately actionable. *Kingdom Strategies for End-Time Prophetic Prayer* is exactly what the Body of Christ needs in this hour. In this book, she connects the spirit and power of Elijah to the Church's assignment right now, creating a strategic manual for those who sense that we are living in the final generation. I'm so grateful that Jenny Eddison faithfully stewarded this message across the finish line. Patsy may have gone home to heaven, but this mandate is still very much alive. Get this book. Pray through it. Share it. The hour demands it.

Alan DiDio
www.revivalnation.com

Kingdom Strategies for End-Time Prophetic Prayer is a timely and biblically grounded message for the body of Christ. Patsy Cameneti, with Jenny Eddison, provide clear insight into the believer's role in partnering with God through Spirit-led prayer to advance His purposes on earth. This book reminds us that prayer is not passive devotion, but strategic cooperation with heaven. With wisdom, balance, and a strong foundation in Scripture, the authors call believers to maturity, spiritual discernment, and alignment with the Holy Spirit as we prepare the way for the Lord and participate in His kingdom work.

Billy Epperhart
CEO, Andrew Wommack Ministries,
Charis Bible College, and GOD TV
Founder, WealthBuilders

For more than 30 years, Patsy Cameneti was not only a dear friend to me, but a trusted prayer partner. I had the privilege of watching her live the message she now leaves behind in this book. Her life was marked by integrity, spiritual authority, discernment, and unwavering devotion to the purposes of God. Now that she has gone home to be with the Lord, this work stands as part of her lasting legacy to the body of Christ.

Kingdom Strategies for End-Time Prophetic Prayer is not a book born out of theory or trend. It is the fruit of decades spent in strategic, Spirit-led intercession. Patsy understood that prayer is not passive devotion. It is partnership with heaven. She carried a deep revelation of our seating with Christ and the authority that flows from alignment under His headship.

Together with Jenny Eddison, she presents a biblically grounded and balanced framework for prophetic prayer in these critical days. This message avoids sensationalism and instead calls believers into maturity, into delegated authority, discernment, and obedience to the Holy Spirit. It brings clarity to spiritual landscapes without fear and anchors everything in Christ's supremacy.

I especially value the way this book reveals the character of God, His justice, mercy, righteousness, and judgment, showing that every expression of His nature flows from His love. Patsy carried a deep confidence in God's goodness, even when addressing serious spiritual matters. That strength and steadiness permeate these pages.

She believed the Church is called to function as the Ecclesia, positioned, watchful, and responsive, praying under divine direction to see God's purposes established on earth. This book calls believers to that higher place of collaboration with heaven. Those who knew Patsy know that she did not speak lightly, pray casually, or move without the unction of the Holy Spirit. This book reflects that same sobriety, authority, and grace.

I wholeheartedly recommend this work to those who desire to move beyond surface level prayer and step into mature, Spirit-directed partnership with God. May this message continue to prepare the way of the Lord and strengthen the Church until the knowledge of His glory fills the earth.

Lynette Hagin
Director, Rhema Bible Training College
Broken Arrow, Oklahoma, USA

Patsy was always a lover of God's deepest mysteries. Her heart was drawn to uncover every facet of truth to be found. She had a way of holding up a lantern and creatively calling us in to discover this beauty for ourselves. I believe this book is a timely road map left to inspire us to find the beauty, intention, and courage of prophetic prayer and its intricate purpose in praying down heaven in these last days.

Lynne Hammond
Living Word Christian Center, Founding Pastor
Brooklyn Park, Minnesota, USA

If there was ever a book written to connect the Church with heaven's purposes, this is it.

The experience, the wisdom and perspective from which *Kingdom Strategies for End-Time Prophetic Prayer* is written will elevate you to new levels of effectiveness in prayer. It is like a master key to give you access to the knowledge that connects you with your divine purpose.

From her youth, Patsy loved praying with our family and others about the end-time move of God on earth. It was a great satisfaction and joy for me to meet Jenny Eddison. I knew Jenny was Patsy's prayer partner whom God was using to carry out this prayer assignment. Thank you, Jenny, for your partnership in prayer with my sister, Patsy, all her years while in Australia. Your collaboration and deep commitment to Patsy's message and legacy can now be fuel for effective end-time prophetic prayer.

The following quote from the book says it well: "Having a wider scope and clearer understanding of all the participants in the spirit realm and on earth really helps when you start working in the spirit from here on earth. It's like getting a map of the town before you go there on vacation. The kingdom of God is found in both the spirit realm and the natural realm. We can become participants in the plan of God as we work together with Him having interface with both realms—natural and spiritual. We work with Him to bring His plans from the spiritual realm to the natural realm. You are literally bringing heaven to earth!"

Trina Hankins
Mark Hankins Ministries
Alexandria, Louisiana, USA

I was so blessed to hear that *Kingdom Strategies for End-Time Prophetic Prayer* has been released. Patsy Cameneti carried a rare blend of prophetic clarity, theological integrity, and tender intimacy with the Holy Spirit—and to see the culmination of much of that wisdom in this book is a sweet joy. For decades, she labored in prayer not for platform, but for the purposes of God to be established on earth.

This book reflects that same depth and maturity. It is not driven by hype or speculation, but by a profound understanding of our seated position in Christ and our sacred invitation to partner with Him in bringing heaven to earth. Patsy understood that prophetic prayer is not striving—it is collaboration. It is hearing what the Spirit is saying and returning it to Him in faith-filled obedience to see His will is done.

In these pages, you will find wisdom for the days we are living in—clarity regarding spiritual authority, discernment concerning the times, and a steady, biblical framework for praying into civil, cultural, and church spheres without fear or sensationalism. This message calls the Church higher—into rest, into alignment, into maturity.

I am especially moved that this work has been brought to completion in honor of Patsy's homegoing. It feels like the continuation of a mission and mantle she carried so faithfully. May this book awaken watchmen, strengthen intercessors, and equip the body of Christ to prepare the way of the Lord with confidence, humility, and joy.

With heartfelt endorsement,
Dr. Katherine Ruonala
Senior Leader
Glory City Church
Brisbane, Australia

This is a message that will particularly resonate with leaders, thinkers, and those who sense a call not merely to respond to spiritual environments, but to help shape them. What makes this work especially meaningful is the fruit of Patsy's and Jenny Eddison's decades-long partnership in prayer. Together they offer insight into the architecture of God's kingdom—His justice, His mercy, His authority, and the role of the Church in stewarding His purposes. They bring understanding specifically in areas not largely spoken about before now. The result is both an invitation and a challenge—to upgrade our understanding and engage with the revelation heaven is releasing from a place of maturity, rest, and spiritual authority. I believe this book comes at an important moment for the Church. In a rapidly shifting world, this message offers both grounding and vision, reminding us that prayer is not merely reactionary but strategic, prophetic, and deeply connected to the heart of God and His grand plan. I am confident this book will serve as a significant resource for leaders and intercessors for many years to come.

Jen Tringale
Author and International Speaker

KINGDOM STRATEGIES

FOR END-TIME

PROPHETIC PRAYER

Harrison House Books by Patsy Cameneti

Kingdom Strategies for End-Time Prophetic Prayer

Engendered: What Was God Thinking? Gender Roles & Relationships

The Spirit Realm: The Place We Work with God in Prayer

The Official Workbook for The Spirit Realm

The Official Summary of The Spirit Realm

KINGDOM STRATEGIES

FOR END-TIME

PROPHETIC PRAYER

BRINGING HEAVEN'S MASTER PLAN TO EARTH

PATSY CAMENETI

WITH JENNY EDDISON

All emphasis within Scripture quotations is the author's own.

Published by Harrison House Publishers
Shippensburg, PA 17257

ISBN 13 TP: 978-1-6675-1464-2
ISBN 13 eBook: 978-1-6675-1465-9

For Worldwide Distribution, Printed in the U.S.A.
1 2 3 4 5 6 7 8 / 30 29 28 27 26

ACKNOWLEDGMENTS

Our daughters, Liliana and Annalisa, and I want to extend a heartfelt thank you to Jenny Eddison for her dedication in bringing *Kingdom Strategies for End-Time Prophetic Prayer* to life.

Jenny, an associate pastor at our Rhema Family Church in Australia, prayed with Patsy almost weekly for twenty years, and they worked closely together on previous books.

Patsy had shared that the Lord mandated her to write two more books, and she diligently worked on *Daily at His Table* and prayed, studied, and documented this project as well. When Patsy went home to be with the Lord in September 2025, our family knew the mandate still had to go forward. The book had to be published.

Jenny rose to the occasion, compiling Patsy's notes and contributing from her years alongside Patsy—praying, sharing, and teaching together.

Our family is grateful to Jenny for bringing the Lord's mandate and Patsy's vision to the printed page.

Tony Cameneti

CONTENTS

FOREWORD

By Annette Capps

Patsy Behrman Cameneti and I met on the first day of classes at Rhema Bible Training Center in September 1976. It was a "divine connection" seemingly organized by random events. To say that she became a "friend" is a vast understatement. There are some things that cannot really be defined—and God-ordained spiritual connections are difficult, if not impossible, to explain.

For the next 49 years, no matter how long it had been since we talked, or how far away we lived from each other, we reconnected at random times destined by God for specific purposes of His kingdom. As odd as it may seem, we simply would pick up where we left off from our last visit. Spiritual connections are like that, outside space and time—eternal.

So, although my dear friend is now in the presence of her Savior and loved ones, she has left us a priceless treasure in the form of this book. It is rich with the deep wisdom that only comes from knowing the *Source* of all wisdom.

Her comparison of spiritual government versus civil government and mercy versus justice is extraordinarily insightful, which has given me a new way to look at modern events. How many of us see things through the filter of our own opinions, seeing things merely from a human point of view, not from God's?

Patsy was acutely aware of the time we are living in, between the first coming of Christ and the second coming of Christ. Just as John the Baptist prepared the way for the first coming, we, the Church, are called to prepare the way for the second coming, which is imminent. How do we prepare the way? In this book, we are given keys and practical training that I believe comes straight from the Holy Spirit. The book concludes with advice and wisdom on beginning and leading a prayer group. (It only takes two. Get started!)

I can personally attest to the character, life, and integrity of Patsy Cameneti. But most of all, I can attest to her profound insight into the nature of God through her intimate relationship with His Son, Jesus Christ. What a legacy she leaves to all of us. May we all rise up to that place of prayer she envisioned, praying from the Father's heart to bring His plans and purposes to pass upon the earth.

Forever grateful,
Annette

PREFACE

By Tony Cameneti

There are many people who knew Patsy as a minister, a teacher, a prayer leader, or a friend.

I knew her as all of those—but first, I knew her as my wife.

For decades, I had the privilege of watching her live out in private exactly who she was in public. There was no separation between platform and home, between pulpit and kitchen table, between ministry and everyday life. She was genuine. Completely authentic. The same in the quiet moments as she was in front of a crowd.

Integrity was not something she preached—it was something she lived.

Patsy was kind in ways most people never saw. She noticed people others overlooked. She listened carefully. She carried burdens quietly. She loved deeply. Whether someone was influential or unknown, strong in faith or struggling, she treated them with the same grace and dignity.

What you hold in your hands is not simply a book of ideas. It is the overflow of a life of prayer.

For years, I watched Patsy seek the Lord when no one else was around. She did not pray to be heard by people—she prayed to hear from God. The insights in these pages were not gathered casually. They were birthed in communion with the Holy Spirit.

Patsy had a remarkable ability to see beyond the surface of events. She believed that the Church must discern the times and respond from heaven's viewpoint, not merely human opinion. She lived with an awareness that we are in a sacred window of time—between Christ's first coming and His soon return. That awareness did not produce fear in her. It produced focus. She believed the Church is not called to react to the world, but to prepare the way for the Lord through prayer, alignment, and obedience.

This book reflects that conviction.

Kingdom Strategies for End-Time Prophetic Prayer carries practical instruction; but more than that, it carries heart. Patsy believed that prayer was not reserved for a few specialists. She believed ordinary believers could gather—even if "only two"—and shift atmospheres, influence communities, and participate in God's purposes on earth.

She envisioned believers rising up, not in noise or self-promotion, but in humble, united, Spirit-led prayer.

As her husband and ministry partner, I can say without hesitation: what she wrote, she lived. Her insight flowed from intimacy with Jesus. Her strength flowed from time in His presence. Her wisdom flowed from knowing the Source.

Her physical voice may now be silent on this earth, but her message continues.

May this book draw you closer to the Father's heart.

May it awaken in you a deeper life of prayer.

And may we all step into the place of partnership with God that she so clearly saw.

With gratitude for her life and legacy.

Tony

INTRODUCTION

By Jenny Eddison

Patsy and I prayed together almost every week for almost 20 years. With us were two other ladies, Edith Szilveszter and Diana Ryan. Early in those days, Patsy heard from God the phrase "Look because there's something to see, listen because there's something to hear." Certainly, over the following 20 years as we prayed together and worked with God, we discovered some amazing things about the spirit realm and the ways of God on earth. He was continually drawing us into closer collaboration with Him.

From our seating in Christ Jesus and the perspective that gives us, we discovered a spiritual landscape and saw the participants in that landscape. We found ourselves praying in the nations of the earth and about things that our minds could never have conceived. We saw with clarity the role of the Church and the outworking of God's justice in the civil arena. All of these things are working together to bring to earth God's master plan for the culmination of the age and the return of Jesus.

And so, the essence of this book grew and took on form just as a babe grows in its mother's womb. This book is not just a Bible teaching on prayer. It's a collection of those things we saw as we prayed, insights into the Word of God, and most of all, a strategic manner of praying as citizens of the kingdom.

It was Patsy's desire that as you read these pages you would not only be encouraged, inspired, and equipped to pray with spiritual intelligence, but also develop such a close relationship with God that you would know His mind, His will, and His heart for the people of every nation, tribe, and tongue.

Over the years it has been my joy and privilege to collaborate with Patsy and curate the contents of this book for publication. Working with God in prayer has been one of the greatest privileges of our lives and for sure it is the most exhilarating!

> But the end and culmination of all things has now come near; keep sound minded and self-restrained and alert therefore for [the practice of] prayer.
>
> —1 Peter 4:7 AMPC

PROPHECY

From Patsy Cameneti

So, the way of the Lord is being made in these days for yea, He will come. He said He would and He will come; this same Jesus will come again. And His way is being made and every mountain is being brought low, every valley brought up, every crooked place straight, and the rough places plain; and yes, the glory of the Lord shall be revealed and all flesh shall see it together for the mouth of the Lord has spoken it.

These are days of great straightening. The crooked things are being straightened. That that has been distorted by wrong thinking is being straightened. That that has been distorted by workings of demons is being straightened by the Spirit of the Lord. That that has been distorted and made crooked by tradition and men's ways is being straightened for the way of the Lord to be made. All shall give way for the straightening of this way in these days. Crooked thinking in the individual will be straightened; things that have distorted relationships are being straightened. That that has divided and that that has driven apart is being straightened in these days.

Yea, the glory of the Lord shall be revealed, but a straightening is coming in these days to make it possible. Let the straightening of God happen in your own life and let straightening words come out of your mouth. That that you see crooked, as the Spirit of the Lord moves upon you, use your tongue to straighten it up. For the way of the Lord must be made and will be made. And He has called an army of women to help Him straighten up some crooked things.... But those who are calling things to be straightened must know that there is a straightening in your own life. Oh, the Spirit of the Lord would straighten up your soul; would straighten up the order of thinking; would straighten up your life.

A great and glorious thing He does and who can stay His hand. For He has ordered these things to be, and so they shall happen, but not just to you. No, they shall happen in you and they shall happen through you for He has ordained that it is through the Church that He will manifest to the principalities and powers His manifold wisdom.

In desiring more of Him, there is only so much a person can contain. To have more, much must be given. To have more, there must be a great giving out for there to be a great influx. So, the Spirit of the Lord does call upon you who have received much, He will require much and you will give it for even as it is written, "His son shall be willing in the day of His power." So, you are willing; you are willing....

Prophecy delivered by Patsy Cameneti
September 2002

PART ONE

SET THE TRAJECTORY FOR PRAYER

Before embarking on any special operations mission, a "special ops" soldier requires clear mission orders and proper operational authority. Working with God in prayer is the same way. Once your purpose is clearly identified, you are able to use God's operational strategies and protocols as well as the delegated authority you are given to help bring God's plans into the earth.

1

THE PURPOSES OF GOD

There is specific significance to this chapter. It is almost prophetic in nature in light of Patsy's homegoing in September 2025. Throughout her life, Patsy knew that she was a participant in the greater continuum of God's purposes and plans. She was a living example of one who focused on the bigger picture rather than solely on her personal gifts and calling. As significant as her life was, she recognized her place within God's overall purpose rather than as a stand-alone figure in ministry. Patsy now has joined the great cloud of witnesses, cheering us on to live in the purposes of God.

—Jenny Eddison, September 2025

Starting Out

In my younger days, I loved to go skiing, both in the snow and on the water. It took some time and practice, and some degree of bravery, but eventually I got to the place where I was not too bad at all!

With waterskiing, when you first start out, you have to get in the water and get into position. You start, up to your neck in water, squatting on the skis and holding the rope for dear life!

Then the boat begins to go. They say, "Just hang on!" And if you just hang on, the boat pulls you up out of the water. For a time, the water hits your face and you are afraid and you are thinking, *Oh my lands! This is not fun.* But if you just hang on and don't let go, a wonderful thing happens—you walk on water!

The purposes of God are much like that. A lot of times we have used all we know about salvation and redemption just to keep our head above water. But, it's so much better to grab on to a divine purpose and rise up out of the water. You may start out thinking, *This is not fun,* but if you keep holding on to God's purpose and look straight ahead, you'll start to discover some of the most amazing things in God. All you need to do is hold on!

Your purpose always pushes you beyond your own abilities and giftings.

Your purpose is always beyond yourself. Your purpose always pushes you beyond your own abilities and giftings. In this walk of faith, you never get to the place where you don't need God.

Not Just for Your Own Benefit

There are things in our life that we can approach Him on—needs or desires—and we go to the Word, and the Holy Spirit takes up together with us on those needs. But there are assignments where God actually enlists your help. He puts it in your heart and He causes you to desire things that He wants. We are most aware of what we want, but it may escape our consideration that actually God wants something. He made us righteous not only for our salvation, but so He can use us in the unfolding of His plans and purposes on earth, not just in our own personal lives. Becoming aware of what He wants, and working with Him on those things, has been the greatest adventure of my life!

I would hate to stand before Jesus and realize I used His great work of redemption for nothing more than staying afloat. We were made for more than just living in personal victory. Aren't you glad that Jesus didn't just come to earth to demonstrate His own personal victory? Yes, He was victorious personally, but His purpose was *our* victory.

Your Life's Purpose

Purpose is essential to life. Without it, life loses meaning. People will seek purpose in various places, such as social interaction, sport, career, travel, and the like. You could write your own list.

Having a clear sense of purpose gives us something to look forward to, but more than that, it provides meaning for our existence that will cause us to persist through the challenges of life. It gives us hope for our final outcome and ultimately, connects us to something greater than ourselves.

When we are born again, we share in the most amazing gift of life—eternal life—and all the benefits that Jesus bought and paid for in His work of redemption. Our new life in Christ Jesus will renew our sense of personal purpose and value. Many of us will find a vocation or a "calling" in God, whether it's a ministry calling, a vocational calling, or a renewed enthusiasm for what we may already be engaged in. Many of us will find that our life now has new meaning and hope for next year, next week, or even just the next day.

There are those who have found purpose for their own life but have not yet seen a purpose that is greater than themselves. When you lose sight of something greater than yourself, *you* become your purpose, and your life becomes only involved with what concerns you. Every word you hear is for you; everything that you receive is for you, but that is *not* the highest potential for your life.

Eternal purpose carries greater value than temporary or earthly purpose. There is a greater reason that you have gotten hold of God and that God has gotten hold of you. You become part of His grand and glorious body, linked to His grand and glorious purpose, which is part of His grand and glorious plan. God has honored us by letting us be part of His greater plan.

God has honored us by letting us be part of His greater plan.

We will never be fulfilled as long as our life is about our own personal victory. When we grab hold of a divine purpose, we still enjoy our salvation—but we discover so much more!

Our Father's Business

I'm so thankful for all that Jesus bought and paid for that I get to enjoy. But there comes a time in our maturing when we ought to realize that we have not come to the kingdom of God just for the benefit of our own life. We have been brought to the kingdom to do something for the kingdom.

I saw this in an old movie from years ago. A businessman was so delighted when his wife had their firstborn son. He was excited to add "...and Son" to the sign over his print shop. That little baby boy was the beneficiary of the prosperity of his father's business, but at a certain age, he would need to make good the additional wording on that building's facade. He would have to actually *be* the "...and Son" his father so proudly had painted all those years ago. He would have to be about his father's business.

Jesus had that realization when He was just 12 years old. He said to his parents, "I must be about my Father's business" (Luke 2:49 NKJV).

Eternal Purpose

Eternal purpose extends way beyond an individual's lifespan. In the context of the 2,000 years since Jesus' work of redemption, a single human life is relatively brief. The saints in the Old Testament who are listed in the "Hall of Faith" in Hebrews knew this and had an eye toward the future that was well beyond their lifespan.

> All these people died still believing what God had promised them. They did not receive what was promised, but they saw it all from a distance and welcomed it. They agreed that they were foreigners and nomads here on earth.
>
> —Hebrews 11:13 NLT

> And all these, having obtained a good testimony through faith, did not receive the promise, God having provided something

> better for us, that they should not be made perfect apart from us.
>
> —Hebrews 11:39-40 NKJV

Those who have gone before, more often than not, never saw what they had been believing God for. They saw something that could only be seen with the eye of faith. In context of these scripture verses, they saw into the future a coming Messiah and lived their lives for that purpose.

However, this spiritual principle extends beyond the Old Testament heroes of faith. It also applies to those in the church age who have gone before us too, that those heroes of faith should not come to perfection apart from us! Our purposes collide eternally.

Can you see that? It's a continuum that goes beyond your own faith for your own life. It goes beyond a person having an individual call for their own life and ministry, even though there is an element of truth about that. Even Paul said, "I've finished my course and have run my race."

The plan and purposes of God are much greater than your short time on this earth. The plan of God actually started at creation and will continue right up to the time when Jesus will reign on earth as King of kings.

Aren't you thankful that your own life is not all that constitutes the plan of God? Our lives can slot in nicely into the plan of God. That's what we're involved in. If I can see beyond myself, I can see something in the distant future that I may not be on earth to experience. It's the final conclusion of that plan. And all these heroes of faith in the Old Testament and even in the church age were able to see beyond themselves. They saw the eternal purposes of God.

We all can live in the eternal purposes of God right now when we live for His purpose. We become part of the continuum of prophets and believers from the Garden of Eden to present day, through the ages to come, and even the end of all ages.

Hebrews 12 goes on to say that those who have gone before us—this great cloud of witnesses—are cheering us on and even working in collaboration with us. They saw the promise from afar off, and now see the end from the beginning just as God does. You could say that these saints who are in heaven are at the end already and they are calling us from the end, "Keep running! You're almost there!"

Communion of Saints

I woke up one night, and I heard something. It was like an announcement on the inside of me. "Communion of Saints." I thought, *What is that? I'm Pentecostal, and that sounds a little Catholic to me.* Yet it resounded in my heart like a bell that keeps reverberating.

I said, "Communion of Saints? What's that?" So I got out of bed, but I didn't pray about it. I Googled it! What I found painted the picture I was seeing in my heart. It's not Catholic; it's a belief that Christians held for centuries. They had a strong conviction of one universal body around the world in heaven and on earth that exists beyond their own experience on earth.

I thought, *That's a revelation we need to not let go of.* I believe the Holy Spirit is ringing that bell again.

> Therefore, since we are surrounded by such a huge crowd of witnesses to the life of faith, let us strip off every weight that slows us down, especially the sin that so easily trips us up. And let us run with endurance the race God has set before us. We do this by keeping our eyes on Jesus, the champion who initiates and perfects our faith. Because of the joy awaiting him, he endured the cross, disregarding its shame. Now he is seated in the place of honor beside God's throne.
>
> —Hebrews 12:1-2 NLT

Called Up

To everything there is a time and a season, and we are in the season now when God has called us to the kingdom for great purpose, and not limited to your own life or within your own lifespan. There is something that you must do for the kingdom. There is something that your personal life can do that will go way beyond your lifespan and into the next dispensation and even into eternity.

When there is a greater cause, it is better that you take up the higher cause and purpose. In pursuing the highest purpose, your home is protected. In pursuing the higher cause, your family is protected. You can spend all of your energy and your life's blood defending yourself and all that is in your house, but if there is a higher cause and you don't defend the higher cause, you'll end up losing it all. Something I know for sure. If I take care of God's business, He takes care of my business.

That is what happened with Esther.

> And Mordecai told them to answer Esther: "Do not think in your heart that you will escape in the king's palace any more than all the other Jews. For if you remain completely silent at this time, relief and deliverance will arise for the Jews from another place, but you and your father's house will perish. Yet who knows whether you have come to the kingdom for such a time as this?"
>
> —Esther 4:13-14 NKJV

There is a higher purpose, an eternal purpose, a purpose greater than the thin line of your residence on earth. There has been a high purpose for every generation; but in this particular generation we are living in, we are being called to look up—to come up. Just like in the military, soldiers can be doing their own thing, but when they get called up, they leave what they are doing and they go to serve a greater call. In serving the greater call of defending their nation, their personal life and family are served and protected.

So, What Is Our Purpose?

What is happening around the world in these days can be so confusing, so dynamic. The rate of change can be frightening as we hurtle into largely unknown territory.

Yet, God has a plan, and He's calling us to work with Him in the unfolding of that plan. For the Old Testament heroes of faith, it was the first coming of the Messiah. For us, it's His second coming. This is the highest purpose we can connect to.

In the same way that John the Baptist prepared a way for the first coming of Jesus, we too can be used of God to prepare the way for Jesus' second coming. In fact, God requires it!

> For Zion's sake I will not hold My peace, and for Jerusalem's sake I will not rest, until her righteousness goes forth as brightness, and her salvation as a lamp that burns. ...I have set watchmen on your walls, O Jerusalem; they shall never hold their peace day or night. You who make mention of the Lord, do not keep silent, and give Him no rest, till he establishes, and till He makes Jerusalem a praise in the earth.
>
> —Isaiah 62:1, 6-7 NKJV

This passage of scripture is not talking about our personal victory. It is for Zion's sake. It is for the kingdom's sake. It is for the purposes of God. We are not to keep silent. We are to hold up the purposes of God, day and night, and give Him no peace until it happens and He makes this place, your church, your city, your nation a praise in the earth for the glory of God.

As you read the following pages of this book, I trust you will find your place in the continuum of the plan and purposes of God, and that you will discover the thrill of cooperating with God in prayer to help unfold His plan on earth as it is in heaven.

2

THE SPIRIT AND POWER OF ELIJAH

It was not in the earthquake, it was not in the fire
It was not in a strong mighty wind
It was not in confusion it was not in desire
It was not in the counsel of men
But in a still small voice
That I heard inside
In a still small voice He guides

–Keith Moore (used with permission)

We are indeed hurtling into a season of great anticipation of the coming of the Lord. Just as His first coming required many details to be unfolded, His second coming will also require even more unfolding details.

The importance of prophetic prayer is also increasingly being recognized. Strategies, both new and old, are being brought out of heaven as God is revealing them to us. He is at work! God is inviting us to work with Him in the unfolding of His plan.

God is inviting us to work with Him in the unfolding of His plan.

We are now living in a day when the fear of God is diminishing, and just like the days of the prophet Elijah, the worship of false gods is increasing. There is something we are to do about that! God has plans already written in heaven to address the days we are living in. So how do we get hold of those plans? Let's take a look at two prophets whose life and ministry are an inspiration to us: John the Baptist and Elijah.

John the Baptist

John the Baptist had a ministry and role in the first coming of Jesus that was of such great importance that Jesus said there was no prophet ever before him who was greater. But John the Baptist didn't call down fire from heaven or do anything really spectacular (John 10:41). Even though he came in the spirit and power of Elijah, John had no major miracles.

A prophecy at the time of John's birth through his father, Zechariah, shows us the importance of John's ministry and his connection directly to Jesus' ministry and purpose on earth.

> And you, little one, shall be called a prophet of the Most High; for you shall go on before the face of the Lord to make ready His ways.
>
> —Luke 1:76 AMPC

> Just as it is written in the prophet Isaiah: Behold, I send My messenger before Your face, who will make ready Your way—a voice of one crying in the wilderness [shouting in the desert], Prepare the way of the Lord, make His beaten tracks straight (level and passable)!
>
> —Mark 1:2-3 AMPC

Mark, in this scripture, was quoting Isaiah, so let's see what Isaiah had to say about road building:

> A voice of one who cries: Prepare in the wilderness the way of the Lord [clear away the obstacles]; make straight and smooth in the desert a highway for our God! Every valley shall be lifted and filled up, and every mountain and hill shall be made low; and the crooked and uneven shall be made straight and level, and the rough places a plain. And the glory (majesty and splendor) of the Lord shall be revealed, and all flesh shall see it together; for the mouth of the Lord has spoken it.
>
> —Isaiah 40:3-5 AMPC

John's ministry was to prepare a highway for Jesus to walk on. In fact, he was to prepare the people for Jesus' ministry on earth. He called for repentance and baptized people to make them ready for Jesus' earthly ministry. In some ways, the highway was people—lifted up, brought down, crooked things made straight, and rough places smooth. All these things can be applied to readying people for the ministry of Jesus.

John and Elijah

There is a second aspect to the ministry of John the Baptist that is also significant. He was to come in the "spirit and power of Elijah."

The Angel that came to Zechariah said this:

> He will be a man with the spirit and power of Elijah. He will prepare the people for the coming of the Lord. He will turn the hearts of the fathers to their children, and he will cause those who are rebellious to accept the wisdom of the godly.
>
> —Luke 1:17 NLT

As we have already mentioned, John had no spectacular elements in his ministry. Even more significant is the fact that John's ministry actually began in the wilderness. Such a remote place is not an ideal place for one to choose to launch a ministry! In the wilderness there's no one to hear you. Could it be that John's primary voice was to the heavenlies and those who dwelt there? Keep all this in mind about John and let's look a little closer at Elijah's ministry where we will see something rather interesting.

Elijah's Zeal for God

In 1 Kings 17:1, Elijah made a bold statement. He said, "There shall not be dew nor rain these years, except at my word" (NKJV). There was no indication God told him to declare that. However, Elijah must have had a revelation of a degree of authority in God, as well as his position as a prophet, to be able to make such a bold declaration and know God was honor-bound to respond to his faith. Isn't that just like our God!

Then, three and a half years after Elijah declared that there would be no rain, God told Elijah to show himself to King Ahab and declare that rain will come (1 Kings 18:1). Elijah went on to draw attention to what was at stake through the calling down of fire on the altar. He threw out the challenge and said, "If the Lord be God, then serve Him" (1 Kings 18:21).

God worked with Elijah to separate Israel from Baal, the god of that region. Baal worship had infiltrated the people of God. They had become so mixed up with the spirit of the world that there was no clear delineation between God's people and the people of Baal. So, Elijah challenged the prophets of Baal. He called down fire out of heaven and triumphed over them.

God's people once again proclaimed that Jehovah is indeed God after witnessing this demonstration of the almighty power of God (1 Kings 18:17-40). Yet we can't see in Scripture that God actually instructed him to do any of that. Even though there was a temporary shift in the land for a time, the worship of Baal wasn't completely eradicated.

Elijah Holds on to God's Promise

Finally, toward the end of 1 Kings chapter 18, we see Elijah praying for the one thing that God *did* promise him, that it would rain. God promised him nothing about the fire out of heaven or any of the other miracles. What God had promised him was rain, but rain was the only thing that didn't happen without persevering prayer! Elijah put his head between his knees, and he called on God. He sent his servant to check for rain six times, but each time there was nothing. Aren't you hopeful to see that even Elijah didn't get an instant answer!

Elijah would never ever let go of the promise until he saw the answer, and he didn't need a huge indication. A cloud the size of a man's hand was enough to send him outrunning the king's chariot to get out of the rain!

James 5:7-8 uses the account of Elijah's prayer for rain to illustrate something that should encourage us. He persevered in prayer! Persevering prayer is what precedes and prepares for the coming of the Lord. That should encourage us all to persevere in prayer and contend for the promise of God.

But that is not the end of the story. There was more to come that took Elijah to the end of himself.

Elijah's Fear

Following what could be said to be the most spectacular and supernatural highlight of his ministry, Elijah came face-to-face with his humanity.

> Elijah was a human being with a nature such as we have [with feelings, affections, and a constitution like ours] ....
>
> —James 5:17 AMPC

The spectacular nature of that event on Mount Carmel certainly unleashed a hornet's nest when Elijah provoked the god, Baal. Jezebel, as queen, was influenced by that god, and she made some startling threats toward Elijah. This mighty man of faith, ran off in fear of a woman! Being so intimidated, Elijah made an amazing confession before the Lord.

> Elijah replied, "I have zealously served the Lord God Almighty. But the people of Israel have broken their covenant with you, torn down your altars, and killed every one of your prophets. I am the only one left, and now they are trying to kill me, too."
>
> —1 Kings 19:10 NLT

What Elijah was intimating was, "Look, Lord, I saw what the people were doing and it wasn't good. It made me mad! In my own zeal, I addressed it. But pity me! I did it all by myself and no one was there to help me! Now my life is in danger!"

This seems to be an acknowledgment by Elijah that he did this *for* God and did it in his own strength and his own zeal.

In the scripture passage in Luke 9:51-56 we see Jesus said something to His disciples that could be almost a commentary on Elijah's approach by his own zeal. When faced with non-acceptance by the Samaritans, the disciples said "Lord, do You want us to command fire to come down from heaven and consume them, just as Elijah did?" Jesus responded with a reprimand by saying "You do not know what manner of spirit you are of. For the Son of Man did not come to destroy men's lives but to save them" (Luke 9:55-56 NKJV).

Obviously, the disciples' approach was prompted by their own zeal, not led by the Spirit. Our own ideas and zeal for dealing with contrary opinions or situations will not result in the full unfolding of God's perfect plan. Let's see how Elijah was led by God to address the spirit of Baal.

Elijah's Commission from God

Elijah's experience on Mount Carmel was the scene of a spectacular display of God's power, and it did have an impact on the nation of Israel. However, with Jezebel still under Baal's influence and she still influencing the nation, the worship of Baal was far from finished. It would have to be completely uprooted. God had something for Elijah to do that would deal with the nation in a much more significant and effective way.

When Elijah was at his lowest, at a point where his own zeal had been exhausted, God began to unfold His mighty plan!

We read in 1 Kings 19:13 (NKJV) that Elijah "wrapped his face in his mantle." Now that's an interesting thing for Elijah to do. If his face was wrapped in his mantle, obviously his eyes were covered. He could not see what was all around him. He could only see the mantle. It was covering his face and probably his other senses too.

When God calls you, your confidence is not in your own abilities.

There are times when we, too, need to cover our faces with our "mantle." A "mantle" could symbolize our divine calling and the empowerment of the Holy Spirit for a specific assignment or ministry. When God calls you, your confidence is not in your own abilities. Neither is it in your assessment of the situation. Your confidence is in His calling and the grace to do it. What your eyes and senses receive may actually be a distraction.

So, Elijah covered his face. And when all he could see was the mantle, or his divine calling and the empowerment that came with that calling, God was able to speak and Elijah heard Him.

Still Small Voice

The characteristics that had so marked Elijah's life up until that point were dramatic demonstrations, powerful supernatural interventions, and assertive confrontations. However, this new assignment from God did not come in a spectacular way with mighty wind, earthquake, or fire. It came in a still small voice. It came in a whisper. Elijah had to be silent and listen for God. And God's voice came to Elijah clearly.

Take note of this. Often it isn't in the exuberant and exciting times that God speaks. It's in the times when we are still, quiet, and ready to hear. This would be God's last directive to this prophet.

God's instruction to Elijah in the "still small voice" was:

> Then the Lord said to him: "Go, return on your way to the Wilderness of Damascus; and when you arrive, anoint Hazael as king over Syria. Also you shall anoint Jehu the son of Nimshi as king over Israel. And Elisha the son of Shaphat of Abel Meholah you shall anoint as prophet in your place. It shall be

> that whoever escapes the sword of Hazael, Jehu will kill; and whoever escapes the sword of Jehu, Elisha will kill."
>
> —1 Kings 19:15-17 NKJV

Elijah was instructed to do three things:

1. Anoint Hazael to be king over Syria.
2. Anoint Jehu to be king over Israel.
3. Anoint Elisha to be prophet in Elijah's place.

Of the three God told Elijah to anoint, Elisha would seem to be the most qualified. The others were ungodly and even foreign; therefore, they seemed to be unlikely candidates. Yet God's anointing empowered them to accomplish His plan beyond their natural ability. That anointing came both directly and indirectly through Elijah. Elijah only personally anointed Elisha to be a prophet in his place. How then was the directive to anoint Hazael and Jehu carried out?

Hazael

Hazael became king of Syria through God's anointing delivered by Elisha, who was himself anointed by Elijah. Hazael was described as a cruel and powerful king who was a major adversary of Israel and Judah. Even though he was anointed to be king by Elisha, he murdered his predecessor and took the throne. Not exactly what you would expect of an "anointed king"! Yet we see in 2 Kings chapters 12 and 13 how God used Hazael, a heathen king, in the judgment of Israel brought on by their worship of Baal.

It was the anointing that gave both Elisha and Hazael their authority to fulfill God's purpose against Baal worship (2 Kings 8:7-13).

Jehu

Jehu, a military leader, was the only one anointed with oil, and he was not even anointed by Elijah or Elisha! Elisha sent a young prophet to perform the act, showing that it is the anointing, not the person, that enables God's purpose (2 Kings 9:1-10).

Jehu had a reputation of being a wild man and he did accomplish his commission—brutally. This can be seen in 2 Kings chapters 9 and 10. He didn't even continue in the ways of the Lord. In fact, the scripture says he refused to turn from sin.

> In this way, Jehu destroyed every trace of Baal worship from Israel. ...But Jehu did not obey the Law of the Lord, the God of Israel, with all his heart. He refused to turn from the sins that Jeroboam had led Israel to commit.
>
> —2 Kings 10:28,31 NLT

Anointing in Different Arenas

In order to achieve God's desire to drive out Baal worship in Israel, it took three people operating in three separate areas of influence.

Elisha was a prophet. Hazael was a king. Jehu was a military leader.

God anointed these three different positions, or we could say "seats of authority," in order to accomplish His objective (1 Kings 19:17 NKJV). And Elijah was to dispense that anointing to those who sat in those seats of authority.

A Wider Reaching Effect

The preparation of the way of the Lord in the "spirit and power of Elijah" is something that will affect all these three areas and other civil arenas as well.

While the fire falling on Mount Carmel was spectacular and captured the attention of many to actually uproot the worship of Baal, Elijah had to collaborate with God's plan. It was a plan initiated by God, not Elijah's own ideas empowered by his own zeal. In this assignment from God, Elijah's purpose extended beyond his own lifespan. He was part of the continuum of God's plan, and it had a much wider scope of influence.

At the same time God is working in the Church and through the Church, He is also working in the nations and through the nations, through their rise and fall, through their leaders, governments, and through their civil authorities. His workings in these civil and even military arenas need to be fueled by our prayer.

Our part is to pray and seek the Lord as He speaks quietly and clearly to us. In this way we work with God as part of His plan that may extend beyond our own life span. Elijah wasn't on earth to see the end result of his prayer, namely the eradication of Baal worship in Israel. That was actually completed by Jehu, who was an ungodly military-minded king.

In our days, in preparing the way for the second coming of the Lord, we can expect to see anointing being dispensed through the prophetic word and prophetic prayer. That anointing will directly affect politics and other areas of authority that are not only related to justice and judgment but also the wider unfolding of the plan of God.

It is not only those who stand behind a pulpit whom God anoints. God will also anoint political leaders along with military and civil authorities.

We will see in the following chapters that there are ways to pray for political leaders even in nations that may not be blessed to have godly leaders. We can pray by the help of the Holy Spirit for an anointing to come upon all kinds of leaders in these days.

Elijah and John the Baptist

One of the main things that links the operation of John the Baptist to Elijah is prophetic prayer. Prophetic prayer in its simplest form is prayer initiated by God, received by His prophets, and directed back to God. It's prayer that administers the anointing of God where He directs. Could it be that the most significant ears that hear this kind of prayer are God Himself and all the hosts of heaven?

There's an interesting scripture in Ephesians.

> [The purpose is] that through the church the complicated, many-sided wisdom of God in all its infinite variety and innumerable aspects might now be made known to the angelic rulers and authorities (principalities and powers) in the heavenly sphere.
>
> —Ephesians 3:10 AMPC

This verse says that the wisdom of God is to be made known to the "angelic rulers and authorities, principalities and powers in the heavenly sphere."

The voice of John the Baptist in the wilderness first engaged in communication to the heavenlies—a voice crying out in the wilderness. After that, people on earth began to resonate with what he was declaring and were gathered to him.

Elijah also had to be still enough to hear God's voice. His primary communication was hearing from heaven in the "still small voice." And his response to that voice required obedience, even though his resulting actions, in the short term, were not as spectacular as those that resulted from his own zeal.

The underlying connection between the two prophets was communication with God and obedience to His directives, which resulted in the plan of God unfolding not by their might, zeal, or power, but by God's Spirit.

> So he answered and said to me: "This is the word of the Lord to Zerubbabel: 'Not by might nor by power, but by My Spirit,' says the Lord of hosts."
>
> —Zechariah 4:6 NKJV

We see the results of the communication that both of these prophets had with God. These results went far wider than their own position and perspective. God was able to use them in ways that went way beyond their own circle of influence and even their own lifespan.

Wider Panorama in Prayer

It is important that as we pray to prepare the way of the Lord in the earth today that our panorama is widened. We cannot have skinny thinking and skinny prayer in these days because the ways of the Lord are very, very broad. God is able to use a wide variety of leaders, influencers, and people in authority to get His plans accomplished in the earth. And He does this in His own unique way.

Don't be surprised at where you see the anointing, and don't be offended on whom you see the anointing. Look for it. You'll see it. The anointing of God is essential for people to do what God has called them to do. You, as a pray-er have been commissioned to dispense it and it will come not by your own zeal, might, or power—but by following after God's direction. Be thrilled whenever you see the anointing, knowing it is all working together to bring heaven's plan to earth.

3

OUR AUTHORITY TO PRAY

Everything in our kingdom is by the will of the Father, for the glory of the Son, empowered by the Holy Spirit, and activated by faith. So when we believe, things move. When we speak in faith, when we act in faith, it activates things in this kingdom.

—Patsy Cameneti, 2015

The Voice

We saw in the previous chapter that John the Baptist had a ministry and role in the first coming of Jesus which was of such great importance that Jesus said there was no prophet ever before him who was greater.

He was a "voice of one crying in the wilderness: 'Prepare the way of the Lord'" (Luke 3:4 NKJV). "In the wilderness…." Why was he out in the wilderness? Who was there to hear him? Initially, not crowds of people. So who heard him?

> John is the man to whom the Scriptures refer when they say, "Look, I am sending my messenger ahead of you, and he will prepare your way before you."
>
> —Matthew 11:10 NLT

> I tell you the truth, of all who have ever lived, none is greater than John [the Baptist]. Yet even the least person in the Kingdom of Heaven is greater than he is!
>
> —Luke 7:28 NLT

Preparing the way initially started with John taking what was in the heavenlies and bringing it to earth with his words. John gave voice to what God was saying, and this created a highway for Jesus to walk on.

> **John gave voice to what God was saying, and this created a highway for Jesus to walk on.**

The sound went out, and eventually people heard it. They responded, repented, and were baptized for repentance. It was his voice that was such a significant part of his ministry, and it was first heard in the heavenlies.

How Can We Be Greater Than John the Baptist?

Jesus said many startling things in His life here on earth. One of those startling things was what he said regarding John the Baptist and those who would be even greater than him!

> I tell you the truth, of all who have ever lived, none is greater than John the Baptist. Yet even the least person in the Kingdom of Heaven is greater than he is!
>
> —Matthew 11:11 NLT

Why was he so great? From before he was even born, the Holy Spirit came upon him until he was filled.

> For he will be great and distinguished in the sight of the Lord. And he must drink no wine nor strong drink, and he will be filled with and controlled by the Holy Spirit even in and from his mother's womb.
>
> —Luke 1:15 AMPC

The Greek word for *filled* in this verse is *pletho,* which means being filled with the Holy Spirit for ministry, suggesting an outward filling for action, distinct from being filled inwardly.

Up until then, the prophets of old had the Spirit of God come upon them but not abide within them or take up residence. But then Jesus says that even the least person in the kingdom is greater than John! Think on that for a bit. *You*, as a citizen of the kingdom of God, are greater than John the Baptist! How could that be? Have you performed any amazing miracles? Have you performed supernatural acts like Elijah? Have crowds of people been drawn to your preaching in the wilderness? Maybe you have, but probably not!

But there is something *in* you that makes you greater. What could that be? Until Jesus' blood was placed on the mercy seat and redemption was made possible for humans, the Spirit of God could not take up residence in a human. The Spirit of God would come *upon* a person, and we read about how they were "anointed" for service. It was part of the mystery to be revealed in the church age—"Christ *in* you, the hope of glory" (Colossians 1:27 NKJV).

Now you are the temple of the Holy Spirit and God has made *you* His dwelling place. He had to get into the earth legally in order to carry out His plans. This happened first through Jesus and then through every believer who ever came after Him.

Your Role Is Essential. God Needs You!

Because God is the righteous and just God, He will not override even His own decrees. God gave authority on the earth to Adam and Eve. He will not rescind their "lease." It's a legal lease. God gave Adam and Eve the commission and the authority to bring the earth into the dominion of God by the words of their mouths.

Adam, however, allowed an illegal entrant to usurp his authority when he submitted to the devil. Now Satan, or the devil, is the "god of this world" (2 Corinthians 4:4 NLT). So in order for God to legally work in the earth, He needs humans to take back the authority He originally gave them. And He needs them to be His mouthpiece on the earth.

A Speaking Spirit

God created everything by the word of His power (Hebrews 11:3). All creation responds to the substance that created it.

My husband and I pastor Rhema Family Church in Australia and direct Bible Schools in Papua New Guinea where there are more than 300 local languages. The language that is most widely used and was formed early in the days of colonization is Pigeon or "Tok Pisin." In the Tok Pisin Bible, the account of creation gives a very unique description of how creation responded to the Voice of God. In the Tok Pisin Bible,[1] Genesis 1:1-7 portions say:

All creation responds to the substance that created it.

"Bihain God i tok olsem" ("Then God He said like this")

"Lait i mas kamup" (Light, it must come up)

"Orait lait i kamup" (Alright, light it came up)

In the following verses in Genesis 1, the same is said about separation of the waters from the earth, separation of waters from dry ground, vegetation growing from the earth, and so on. God spoke and creation responded.

What a wonderful description of how creation responded to the word of God! "Alright, I will!" (Orait, i kamup) Creation will respond to the substance that created it. That is the voice or the word of God.

"Well, that's God's voice," you may say. But here's the deal. When God created Adam, the Bible says in most translations that God made him a "living being" (Genesis 2:7 AMPC). But the literal translation from the Hebrew is "a speaking spirit." God created Adam to be a "speaking spirit" in His own image.

1 The Bible in Tok Pisin, Papua New Guinea, Bible Society of Papua, New Guinea; https://www.bible.com/versions/3481-tpipng-buk-baibel-long-tok-pisin; and https://www.bible.com/bible/3481/GEN.1.TPIPNG; accessed January 19, 2026.

Speaking Spirit

Genesis 2:7

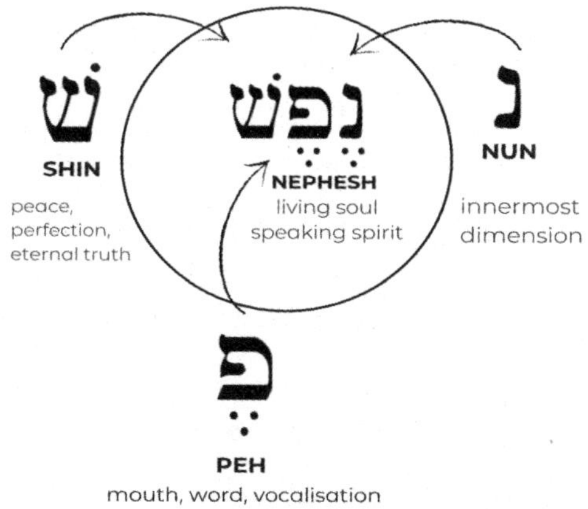

The Hebrew word for *living being* in that verse is *nephesh,* and is made up of three Hebrew words: נֶ פֶ שׁ

These three Hebrew words mean:

שׁ (Shin) peace, perfection, eternal truth

פֶ(peh) mouth, word, vocalisation

נֶ(nun) Inner most, inner dimension

The literal translation when each of these words or letters are put together is "deep, eternal truth, mouth." Adam was created to be a deep, eternally true, mouth. He was literally a speaking spirit.

You could say Adam was to be the mouth of God in the earth. We see in Genesis 2:19 that Adam used his words to have dominion. For example, he called the animals by name, and that's what they became (Genesis 2:20).

We were created to be the mouth of God in the earth. We are to use God's Word to take dominion, and His word in our mouths will cause creation to respond. This is what Paul calls the "word of faith." We have that word and so we speak (2 Corinthians 4:13).

The catch is that we must use God's words. Our own words are idle and ineffective as far as unfolding the plan of God. Our own words do have a degree of power and can produce effects, but for unfolding the plan of God and bringing heaven to earth, we must use God's words and use them in the context of His design and plan.

Jesus gave very clear delineation regarding what we say when we pray.

> I will give you the keys of the kingdom of heaven; and whatever you bind (declare to be improper and unlawful) on earth must be what is already bound in heaven; and whatever you loose (declare lawful) on earth must be what is already loosed in heaven.
>
> —Matthew 16:19 AMPC

The words we use must be what is written and declared either lawful or unlawful in heaven. If the words are not lawful, originating from heaven, they are not going to be effective in unfolding the plan of God. In fact they could actually be working contrary to God's plan and His will. It's going to be unprofitable to go decreeing and declaring something if it's not words that originate in heaven and backed up by the Word of God.

What amazing potential God's words have in our mouth. In this way, we can actually be greater than John the Baptist and even the prophets of old. We have access to far more of God's plan in the Word of God. By the help of the Holy Spirit, as born-again believers we "...have the mind of Christ (the Messiah) *and* do hold the thoughts (feelings and purposes) of His heart" (1 Corinthians 2:16 AMPC).

God's words in our mouth carry great weight; and when spoken, cause all creation to respond. But how do we know what to say? Let's look a bit more into how that operation can take place.

4

SAY WHAT YOU SEE

We're watchers in God. We're facilitating and we're conducting the works of God that have been established. We're facilitating and conducting them through prayer in the Holy Ghost, through inspired utterance. And He needs us to keep speaking what He tells us to speak, because it makes a route for those works to be accomplished that are already settled in heaven. They're to be manifested on the earth.

—Patsy Cameneti, 2022

Previously we saw that speaking God's words can be as powerful as when He speaks them Himself. Many of us are disciplined to speak God's word over our own lives. We know that "Death and life are in the power of the tongue…" (Proverbs 18:21 NKJV). So most of us will guard the words we speak.

The Bible is full of promises for provision, health, and salvation. These are truths we can confidently speak with faith, knowing God is faithful to perform His word.

However, some issues aren't directly covered by a specific promise or verse. These things are hidden in God's mind and need to be sought out. God cares about every detail of your life. Your work, family, home, relationships, and even your small details are important to Him. He has plans and strategies for your life. Even beyond that, He cares about your nation and government, desiring all people to be saved.

God has something to say about everything, so to pray in line with His plans, we must seek Him. The words we speak in prayer are important. We can shape our world, speaking what we believe, having faith in His will for every situation. Faith begins where the will of God is known.

> By faith we understand that the worlds [during the successive ages] were framed (fashioned, put in order, and equipped for their intended purpose) by the word of God, so that what we see was not made out of things which are visible.
>
> —Hebrews 11:3 AMPC

Jesus showed His disciples how to pray in Matthew 6:10 (NKJV). He said, "Your kingdom come. Your will be done on earth as it is in heaven."

God uses our words to bring His will to pass on earth.

Obviously, God's will already exists in heaven. But God uses our words to bring His will to pass in the earth. They are His words, and His words are words that create.

Jesus Saw His Father

The Gospel of John records Jesus saying that He did nothing without first getting it from His Father.

> Then Jesus answered and said to them, "Most assuredly, I say to you, the Son can do nothing of Himself, but what He sees the Father do; for whatever He does, the Son also does in like manner."
>
> —John 5:19 NKJV

> I can of Myself do nothing. As I hear, I judge; and My judgment is righteous, because I do not seek My own will but the will of the Father who sent Me.
>
> —John 5:30 NKJV

> Then Jesus said to them, "When you lift up the Son of Man, then you will know that I am He, and that I do nothing of Myself; but as My Father taught Me, I speak these things."
>
> —John 8:28 NKJV

Even Jesus, as perfect as He was, did nothing and said nothing apart from what He saw or heard from His Father. In that way, He always conformed to His Father's will, and His Father confirmed His words with signs following.

The Mind of God

The apostle Paul writes that we do not know how to pray as we ought to.

> So too the [Holy] Spirit comes to our aid and bears us up in our weakness; for we do not know what prayer to offer nor how to offer it worthily as we ought, but the Spirit Himself goes to meet our supplication and pleads in our behalf with unspeakable yearnings and groanings too deep for utterance.
>
> —Romans 8:26 AMPC

With our own minds, we cannot pray effectively. There is much about God we cannot fathom in our understanding. He dwells in the secret place. However, we do have access to the mind of God through the Holy Spirit Who sounds the very depths of God.

> But it was to us that God revealed these things by his Spirit. For his Spirit searches out everything and shows us God's deep secrets. …For, "Who can know the Lord's thoughts? Who knows enough to teach him?" But we understand these things, for we have the mind of Christ.
>
> —1 Corinthians 2:10,16 NLT

Our Authority and Our Perspective

Jesus didn't just leave us a good example of how to pray. He also gave us a seat of authority from which we pray. But there's even more to that. Our seating in heavenly places gives us the perspective from which we see things.

> And He raised us up together with Him and made us sit down together [giving us joint seating with Him] in the heavenly sphere [by virtue of our being] in Christ Jesus (the Messiah, the Anointed One).
>
> —Ephesians 2:6 AMPC

The secret is looking to God just as Jesus did. He did what He saw His Father do. Where did He see that? It wasn't with His natural eyes. Jesus was a human like us on the earth, but Jesus didn't see His Father with His natural eyes. As He spoke with His Father, He saw with His spiritual eyes.

The Prayer of Faith

The philosopher Archimedes declared, "Give me a place to stand and I will move the earth." Similarly, our position with Christ in the heavenlies gives us authority and perspective to impact the world. With faith as our lever and God's Word as the fulcrum, we can move even the heaviest loads. The key is having the right word from God. Jesus said He would give us the keys to the kingdom, enabling us to unlock and shift even impossible situations.

Watch to See What God Says

Many times we are confronted with things we see with our physical eyes. God often will use things we see, both in the media and in real life, to provoke us to pray.

You see things through your natural eyes, but God takes your natural eyesight and gives you spiritual perspective. You will actually see things on the earth through His eyes and listen for God's voice on the matter.

The prophet Habakkuk saw something coming. He saw the invading army of the Chaldeans coming to attack. This could have led to a logical response of questioning or even challenging God. But before he did anything, he said to God:

> [Oh, I know, I have been rash to talk out plainly this way to God!] I will [in my thinking] stand upon my post of observation and station myself on the tower or fortress, and will watch to see what He will say within me and what answer I will make [as His mouthpiece] to the perplexities of my complaint against Him.
>
> —Habakkuk 2:1 AMPC

"Give me a place to stand and I will move the world" Archimedes

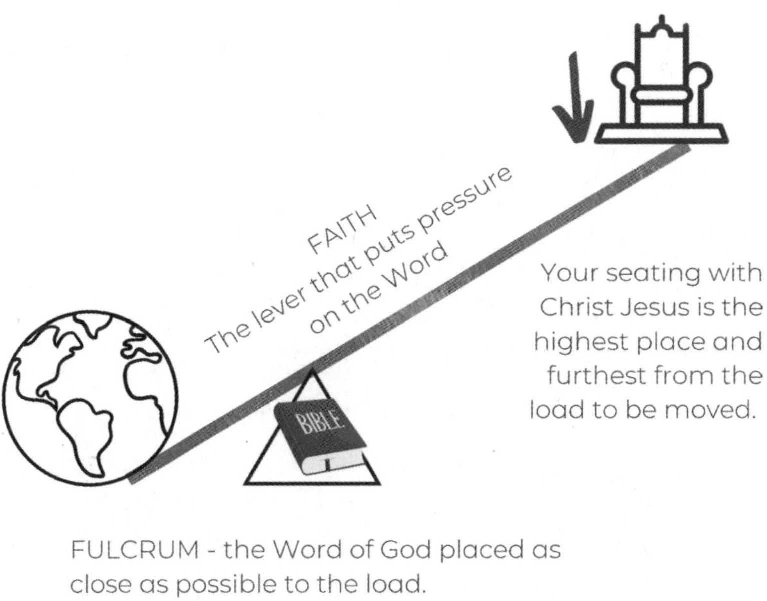

Habakkuk was facing a very challenging event on the horizon. So he ascended to his watchtower—his post of observation—not to see what the Chaldeans would do but to see what God was saying about it. When God showed Habakkuk that the Chaldeans were about to invade, Habakkuk took it back to God. He watched to see what God would say about the matter that he saw. Then what God said would be what Habakkuk would say as His mouthpiece.

Habakkuk knew his purpose: not just to ask God for protection or safety but to serve as God's mouthpiece, bringing divine plans into reality. God's intentions were much greater than personal or national comfort.

Look! There Is Something to See

Sometimes it's not things we see with our natural eyes that move us to pray. The Holy Spirit will also draw us. Even then, we don't know how to pray or what to pray for, as we've already seen in Romans 8:26. When we are in fellowship with God, worshiping Him, the Holy Spirit will speak and we will "see" things. We may sense something, or words may come up as we pray in tongues.

WHAT DO YOU SEE?

God will use your imagination to show you what He wants you to say.

Often in our prayer groups at church I may ask someone, "What are you seeing?" At first they may say, "Nothing," but then I will say "What do you think you saw?" Inevitably, they will say, "I think I saw…." God will use your imagination to show you what He wants you to say.

An example is that of the prophet Jeremiah. In Jeremiah chapter 1, we see that God had appointed Jeremiah to be an overseer to the nations.

> See, I have this day appointed you to the oversight of the nations and of the kingdoms to root out and pull down, to destroy and to overthrow, to build and to plant.
>
> —Jeremiah 1:10 AMPC

That's one huge commission—to root out and pull down, destroy and overthrow. What a formidable task for such a young man. How was he to do that?

Let's see what God's strategy was for him.

> Moreover, the word of the Lord came to me, saying, Jeremiah, what do you see? And I said, I see a branch or shoot of an almond tree [the emblem of alertness and activity, blossoming in late winter]. Then said the Lord to me, You have seen well, for I am alert and active, watching over My word to perform it.
>
> —Jeremiah 1:11-12 AMPC

Can you imagine Jeremiah answering God when he was asked what he saw? "I see the branch of an almond tree." Is that an earth-shattering observation? Surely not! But God said, "Well done, Jeremiah!" I can just imagine Jeremiah scratching his head thinking, *How is that going to root out, pull down, overthrow or destroy anything?*

Although what Jeremiah saw seemed insignificant, God was pleased. By simply saying what he saw, Jeremiah allowed God to act according to His plan, regardless of whether Jeremiah understood the meaning.

A few verses later God asks Jeremiah again, "What do you see?" (Jeremiah 1:13). Jeremiah answered, "I see a boiling pot, and it is facing away from the north." God goes on to tell Jeremiah what the meaning of that boiling pot would be.

You may see something with your spiritual eyes and not understand it. But then you may see something again, and somehow you know what it is. In either case, return it to God. That's all you need to do.

You may say, "How do I know what I'm seeing is right?" Well, God will use things you may see with your natural eyes in the media or in real life, or He may show you something through having a sense of it in your heart. You may see something in your imagination when you are praying. God can use any of these ways, and you don't need to be the one to determine if it's right or not (Romans 8:26-28).

What if you happen to get it wrong? Well, God will surely forgive you for praying anyway! Be assured, the Holy Spirit will ensure only your prayers that are in line with God's will are translated to heaven. If you're not sure about it, return it to God. You don't need to Google it or call your pastor or your best friend. Tell God about it. He will make it clear to you what you are to do with it.

Spiritual Words with Spiritual Language

When we pray, we can expect to see or hear things. Some people see things, some people "hear in their heart." When you pray in tongues especially, your mind doesn't produce anything, so what you see or hear in your imagination is more often a product of your spirit, being led by the Holy Spirit (1 Corinthians 14:14).

When you pray led by the Holy Spirit, He gives you words to say. Praying in tongues is one of the most simple and accurate ways to access the heart of God. When you pray in tongues, you're unlocking the perfect will of God and bringing it into the earth.

When you reach into the realm of the spirit with the help of the Holy Spirit, the words you get are eternal. They can be words in an unknown tongue or words in a language you understand. Either way, you are working with eternal words that simply need to be spoken. When you speak those eternal words, the plan of God makes its earth connection.

> And we are setting these truths forth in words not taught by human wisdom but taught by the [Holy] Spirit, combining and interpreting spiritual truths with spiritual language [to those who possess the Holy Spirit].
>
> —1 Corinthians 2:13 AMPC

You can also ask Him for the interpretation, and He will show you things to come. You will start to see and hear things that come directly from the Spirit of God through your imagination.

> Therefore, the person who speaks in an [unknown] tongue should pray [for the power] to interpret and explain what he says.
>
> —1 Corinthians 14:13 AMPC

That interpretation may come directly or you may just sense or know what it is. Often that interpretation may be walked out by you or someone else in the days and years to come. But your prayer will always produce results.

Circle of Prayer

> For from Him and through Him and to Him are all things. [For all things originate with Him and come from Him; all things live through Him, and all things center in and tend to consummate and to end in Him.] To Him be glory forever! Amen (so be it).
>
> —Romans 11:36 AMPC

There is a circular way of thinking that is very much part of an Eastern mindset. We, as Western minds, Greek-influenced thinkers, see things in a linear way from start to finish. But Eastern or Hebrew culture sees things in a circular way. Things have a beginning, and the end is at the same place as the beginning. That's how Jesus can be the Alpha and the Omega all at once.

Jesus' disciples were often confused about what Jesus said to them, but when He said He came from the Father and was returning to the Father, they responded "Ah! Now we understand."

> "I came forth from the Father and have come into the world. Again, I leave the world and go to the Father." His disciples said

> to Him, "See, now You are speaking plainly, and using no figure of speech!"
>
> —John 16:28-29 NKJV

Prayer starts with God and must be returned to God for it to produce effective outcomes.

> So shall My word be that goes forth from My mouth; it shall not return to Me void, but it shall accomplish what I please, and it shall prosper in the thing for which I sent it.
>
> —Isaiah 55:11 NKJV

Words that are sent from God must be returned to Him in order for them to be effective.

Be that voice crying out in the wilderness. Send your prayers back to God. Complete that circle of prayer, and as you grow and develop in that, God will give you more to see and more to say and maybe even more to do. Just like He said to Jeremiah He will say to you, "I am watching over my word to perform it." Your report to Him gives Him access and a place to work in the earth.

You Are a Watchman

Faith speaks. And your voice carries faith. You say what He shows you from that lifted-up place.

> But if the watchman see the sword come, and blow not the trumpet, and the people be not warned; if the sword comes and takes any person from among them, he is taken away in his iniquity; but his blood will I require at the watchman's hand.
>
> —Ezekiel 33:6 NKJV

Watchmen were tasked with raising alarms about potential threats by sounding a trumpet and informing leaders, not interacting with others or leaving their post. Their role was to warn; if they did so and leaders failed to act, responsibility shifted to the leaders. However, their silence made watchmen liable for any resulting harm.

Brother Kenneth E. Hagin's visions of three black frogs crossing the United States of America highlighted the same idea: when the Church failed to warn, it became responsible for the disturbances that followed. We must not abandon our watch.[2]

Watchmen guarded city walls, warning people of threats. In prayer, spiritual watchmen see into the spirit and wait on God to see what He would say. Like nerves relaying messages to the brain, watchers communicate vital information so responses can be coordinated by God.

Report to the Head

> My eyes bring suffering to my soul....
>
> —Lamentations 3:51 NKJV

Your eyes influence your heart, so it's important to guard them, both naturally and spiritually, if you want to see clearly and be an effective watcher. Don't be a watcher who has matter or rubbish in your eyes. If you entertain your eyes with things that you are going to have to take authority over later, your eyes are not going to be sharp. We want to be sharp and alert.

My husband, Tony, and I have a friend who works in the Australian Navy in the submarine corps. His job is simply to watch and report. They listen for any communication and are on the lookout for maritime vessels. Then they simply report what they see to head base. In doing that, they keep the nation guarded and protected. It's not their role to send out any torpedoes or drop any bombs. The Navy generals and those in charge make decisions on action that needs to be taken and send commands to other parts of the Navy to carry out.

---

2 Kenneth E. Hagin, "The Triumphant Church," September 30, 2014; accessed January 19, 2026.

Circle of Prayer

Isaiah 55:11 NKJV
So shall My word be that goes forth from My mouth; It shall not return to Me void,
But it shall accomplish what I please, And it shall prosper in the thing for which I sent it.

I heard a line in a movie about this type of military watching and gathering of intel. The commander over a team of "watchers" said, "Our job is not to solve the puzzle. We simply find the pieces and send them on up the chain."

When we watch from our seat of authority and perspective, God will make sure we find what He wants us to see and He will give us words to send the pieces back to Him. He is watching over His word to perform it!

PART TWO

SPIRITUAL LANDSCAPE

If you were to travel to a new city or region, it would be very helpful for you to have a map so you could scan the landscape of that region and be prepared for what you may encounter. Much like visiting an unfamiliar region, the spirit realm is a real place where real beings live and move. They also interact with those who are on earth. It's a dynamic interface that requires some spiritual intelligence.

5

FOUNDATIONAL WORLDVIEW

There is a realm that is real even though it is not seen by the naked eye. There are beings in that realm that can be engaged with, but you can't reach out and touch with your physical hand, though they are not any less real. As surely as we live in this physical and natural realm, there is a spirit realm that was in existence before the world was ever created and it still operates today.

—Patsy Cameneti, *The Spirit Realm*, 2024

Biblical Worldview

As believers, whether we realize it or not, we've already had entrance into the spirit realm. When we are born again, our spirits become alive to God. Everything changes. As we become more aware of who we are in Christ Jesus, we begin to see everything, especially earthly matters, through a unique lens. We call this new perspective a "biblical worldview."

We recognize that what we see around us, such as governments, nations, ethnic groups, and even timelines, is not all that exists. There is much more. These earthly operations—people, groups, timelines—are influenced by the realm of the spirit, for good and for evil.

Having a biblical worldview means looking at life through the Word of God (the Bible) and God's perspective. This worldview affects how we make sense of the world and the spiritual realm that influences us. Instead of following cultural trends and social opinions, we see things through biblical truth, which impacts not only how we live but how we approach prayer.

Stepping Through the Gate

The spiritual landscape in which we operate is a fascinating realm, and we have been given a place in that realm. Jesus is the only sanctioned way to access the realm of the spirit. Of course, the spirit realm is vast and eternal, and a complete understanding of that landscape will take all of eternity to unravel. But we are given a promise that by the Holy Spirit we are able to sound out the depths of God (1 Corinthians 2:9-11).

Jesus is the only sanctioned way to access the realm of the spirit.

When we pray and work in the realm of the spirit, we go in and out and find pasture through Jesus, who is the Gate.

> Yes, I am the gate. Those who come in through me will be saved. They will come and go freely and will find good pastures.
>
> —John 10:9 NLT

Spiritual Landscape

If you were to go on vacation to a particular town, and go there regularly enough, you will get to know the landscape of the town, the streets, the buildings, and even the people who live and work there. The spiritual realm is much like that. We go there, not just once a year for vacation. We can go there every day, freely! And we get to know the landscape of that territory. There are beings in that realm, and those beings influence the people living on the earth. Each group, either in heaven or on earth, operates in unique ways.

Recognizing different beings and their functions will help us avoid ineffective and inappropriate interactions. While our knowledge is never complete, acknowledging what we perceive provides valuable insight and perspective.

> Now we see things imperfectly, like puzzling reflections in a mirror, but then we will see everything with perfect clarity. All that I know now is partial and incomplete, but then I will know everything completely, just as God now knows me completely.
>
> —1 Corinthians 13:12 NLT

EARTHLY AND SPIRITUAL PARTICIPANTS

Within the total landscape on earth and in heaven, there are many different players, both natural and spiritual. These include:

- Groups of people in civil, political, and national arenas, each with distinct roles and responsibilities.
- Nations and ethnic groups, each contributing unique perspectives and functions.
- The Church or the Ecclesia of Jesus Christ. We must never underestimate the effect we as the Church have in the spiritual landscape.
- Spirit beings, which can be either divine or corrupt, influencing events and outcomes.
- Demons that seek to aggravate and disrupt human activity.

In the heavenlies, or the realm of the spirit, there are many beings, all very real and all very active. Some of these beings work under direction of God, some are rebels and are corrupt.

All these participants, whether human or spiritual, work together and fit within the broader plan of God. Seeing how each group operates and intersects can help us work within the ways of God and keep us in line with His plans. Truth gives us secure tracks to run on.

KINGDOM PARTICIPANTS

In the kingdom of God, there are many participants both in the spirit realm and on earth. The kingdom of God is where God reigns and these participants function under His rulership. The Church is part of this kingdom with Jesus as the Head. The following passage of scripture lists the members of the kingdom, both in heaven and on earth.

> But you have come to Mount Zion and to the city of the living God, the heavenly Jerusalem, to an innumerable company of angels, to the general assembly and church of the firstborn who are registered in heaven, to God the Judge of all, to the spirits of just men made perfect, to Jesus the Mediator of the new covenant, and to the blood of sprinkling that speaks better things than that of Abel.
>
> —Hebrews 12:22-24 NKJV

This passage gives us a concise list of those participants who not only are part of God's kingdom but who also work together with us in kingdom business. Let's take a brief look at each.

MOUNT ZION: THE CITY OF THE LIVING GOD

The City of God. Mount Zion. The heavenly Jerusalem. It's a real place in a real realm—the spirit realm. It's not like Mount Sinai that was the place of the Law. Mount Zion is accessed by the blood and the finished work of Jesus, not by fulfilling legal requirements. The writer of Hebrews emphasizes Mount Zion's defining characteristic: its inhabitants. In partnering with God spiritually, it's common to be aware of other beings in His presence who inhabit Mount Zion. Let's examine these groups further.

AN INNUMERABLE COMPANY OF ANGELS

Angels work with God and live in God's presence, free from fear and sadness as they are in "festal gathering." They often said, "Fear not" when appearing to people in the Bible. Their ministry continues today as they provide protection and guidance, especially as events draw closer to Jesus' return.

Assembly of God's firstborn children, whose names are written in heaven.

ASSEMBLY OF GOD'S FIRSTBORN

The Church, as Christ's body, includes all New Testament believers worldwide whose names are written in heaven—both those on earth and those already in heaven. In prayer, you may sense a deep connection before even meeting in person. God's work involves collaboration with any member of His body at any time. The connection can be so real that you sense that you are all in the "same room." Like military branches uniting, believers from different denominations and camps will join in prayer, working together as God directs. The more you pray for God's purposes, the more you become aware of this spiritual teamwork.

GOD HIMSELF

Healthy prayer means coming directly to God, aligning ourselves with Him before continuing our work. Just as musicians tune their instruments to a true pitch before performing, we must seek God—our true pitch and righteous Judge—to stay aligned with Him and aligned with His path for us. God alone is the righteous judge over all things.

THE SPIRITS OF THE RIGHTEOUS ONES MADE PERFECT

Jesus' sacrifice secured eternal redemption for people both before and after the Cross. Those people in Old Testament times were credited with righteousness for their faith as they, by faith, were able to dip into the coming age of grace and take hold of salvation brought by Jesus. Through Jesus' blood, their spirits are now made perfect and they now reside in Mount Zion, the heavenly Jerusalem. They are part of the great cloud of witnesses cheering us on from the grandstand of heaven.

JESUS, THE ONE WHO MEDIATES THE NEW COVENANT
Jesus is our High Priest, and He has been given a ministry that is far superior to the old priesthood. He is the One who mediates for us a far better covenant with God, based on better promises. He is the One who authors anything we do with Him in faith and also the One who finishes and brings those things to completion. As the Mediator of our covenant with God, Jesus guides us by the Holy Spirit to fully understand and benefit from this relationship and to bless others through it. Hebrews contrasts the old and new covenants, showing that the new, led by Jesus our High Priest, offers a superior ministry and better promises (Hebrews 8:6-10 NLT).

THE SPRINKLED BLOOD, WHICH SPEAKS OF FORGIVENESS
The blood of Jesus is central in the context of Mount Zion and the new covenant, representing mercy and forgiveness and the power to overcome sin and guilt. Unlike animal sacrifices of the old covenant, Jesus' blood was absolutely perfect, uncontaminated with sin. His blood offers redemption and mercy, teaching believers to approach God with humility and confidence. Through this new covenant, prayer becomes a privilege and a means to share God's love and forgiveness rather than condemnation.

Three Groups of People on Earth

God sees all mankind and desires for all mankind to be saved. In this age, according to 1 Corinthians 10:32, all the people of the earth are grouped into three different groups: the Jews, the Nations/Gentiles, and the Church.

From the nations of the earth, God separated out for Himself a group of people who came to be His own people—the Hebrews or the Jews as we know them today. All the other nations worshipped other gods, but Jehovah's portion were the children of the promise given to Abraham (Deuteronomy 7:6; 14:2).

From out of those two groups of people God formed the Church or Ecclesia—a new group of people in the earth.

> For Christ himself has brought peace to us. He united Jews and Gentiles into one people when, in his own body on the cross, he broke down the wall of hostility that separated us. He did this by ending the system of law with its commandments and regulations. He made peace between Jews and Gentiles by creating in himself one new people from the two groups. ***Together as one body, Christ reconciled both groups to God by means of his death on the cross***, and our hostility toward each other was put to death.
>
> —Ephesians 2:14-16 NLT

The first groups listed in this verse are the Jews. These are the descendants of Abraham, Isaac, and Jacob.

Next, we see the Gentiles (or Nations, sometimes called Greeks), which include all non-Jewish ethnicities.

Finally, there is the Church of the living God (Ecclesia), which can comprise both Jews and non-Jews who are "born again."

If you've been born again, you're actually a whole different species of human. You are a new creation (2 Corinthians 5:17). When you were first born as a baby, you were born into Adam's race, and you were born into a nation or ethnic group. You have a national identity that is of this earth; but when you were born again, you were born into Christ and into this new nation of Christ's Ecclesia, which is part of the kingdom of God.

You actually hold dual citizenship. You are a citizen of your birth nation and a citizen of the kingdom of God.

> For our citizenship is in heaven, from which we also eagerly wait for the Savior, the Lord Jesus Christ.
>
> —Philippians 3:20 NKJV

It is our function as the body of Christ in the earth to pray for these three groups, or we could say in these three arenas. And when we do our job, all the people groups get blessed as a result of answered prayer. When the Church prays, God will direct the power where it needs to go.

You are a citizen of your birth nation and a citizen of the kingdom of God.

Two Great Events on God's Calendar

Throughout the history of humanity, there have been many significant moments that shaped earth's timeline. However, two events stand out as the two greatest events on God's calendar. These two pivotal moments

Three Groups of People

Give none offence, neither to the Jews,
nor to the Gentiles,
nor to the church of God.
1 Corinthians 10:32 KJV

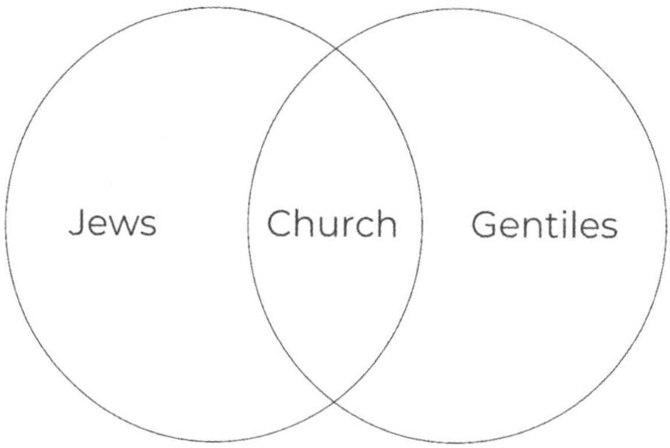

not only define the history of mankind but also give us anchor points in our spiritual life.

JESUS' FIRST COMING

The first great advent on God's calendar was the first coming of Jesus. This was a key event foreseen by Old Testament prophets.

This first advent not only marks a significant time in history, it also marks a significant time in our personal lives and is an anchor point for us.

JESUS' SECOND COMING

Now, as New Testament believers, our gaze is fixed on His return, which we call the Second Coming, as described in Acts 1:11.

Anticipating Jesus' return serves as a guiding anchor, helping us stay aligned with God's purposes. Just as a guitar string is tuned between two secure points to maintain harmony, this coming event will help keep our lives pure before God (1 John 3:3; 2 Timothy 4:8).

A Map for Working in the Kingdom

As we go in and out of the realm of the spirit, we become very familiar with the landscape. Many believers are not even aware of this potential, but some go in and out all the time. They become very aware of the spirit realm and work with the participants and residents of both heaven and earth.

Having a wider scope and clearer understanding of all the participants in the spirit realm and on the earth really helps when you start working in the spirit from here on earth. It's like getting a map of the town before you go there on vacation. The kingdom of God is found in both the spirit realm and the natural realm. We can become participants in the plan of God as we work together with Him having interface with both realms—natural and spiritual. We work with Him to bring His plans from the spiritual realm to the natural realm. You are literally bringing heaven to earth!

6

KINGDOMS AND ANCIENT THRONES

Our Father and the spirits who represent Him in holiness and love are not the only spirits in the spirit realm. In that vast realm, our Father's kingdom is one of light. But there is also a kingdom of darkness whose lord, also a spirit, is unspeakably evil and through deception. There are clear, well-lit ways of working with God in the spirit, and He wants all His children to know them.

—Patsy Cameneti, *The Sprit Realm*, 2024

I have a prayer group with three precious friends, and we have worked together in prayer for almost 20 years. Some years ago, we found ourselves praying for and over the nations of the earth when a phrase came to us: "Ancient Thrones." As we raised this in prayer over subsequent weeks and months, the Lord began to reveal aspects of these ancient thrones, and we started to see patterns in Scripture that began to unfold for us and give clarity on this phrase.

Principalities and Powers

The apostle Paul had remarkable insight into the spiritual realm. He saw with almost X-ray precision how Jesus conquered that realm and all the beings who inhabit the realm of the spirit. Paul writes about how the Father raised Jesus and gave Him a seat far above all principalities, powers, thrones and dominions in the heavenly sphere.

> For it was in Him that all things were created, in heaven and on earth, things seen and things unseen, whether thrones, dominions, rulers, or authorities; all things were created and exist through Him [by His service, intervention] and in and for Him.
>
> —Colossians 1:16 AMPC

> And [so that you can know and understand] what is the immeasurable and unlimited and surpassing greatness of His power in and for us who believe, as demonstrated in the working of His mighty strength, which He exerted in Christ when He raised Him from the dead and seated Him at His [own] right hand in the heavenly [places], far above all rule and authority and power and dominion and every name that is named [above every title that can be conferred], not only in this age and in this world, but also in the age and the world which are to come. And He has put all things under His feet and has appointed Him the universal and supreme Head of the church [a headship exercised throughout the church].
>
> —Ephesians 1:19-22 AMPC

Paul did more than gaze into a spiritual realm. He identified those principalities, powers, thrones, and dominions (Colossians 1:16; Ephesians 6:12).

The terms *principalities, powers, thrones* and *dominions* appear throughout Scripture, notably in Romans 8:38, Ephesians 3:10, Ephesians 6:12, and Colossians 2:15. These words describe elements of the scope, function, and influence of these spirit beings. These words refer to their operation rather than describing four different types of spirit beings or their rankings. These spirit beings have exercised certain influence, power, and dominion, even operating as "gods of this world."

In the book of Daniel, we read about the "prince of Persia" and the "prince of Greece." These entities are spoken of as regional spiritual rulers who had taken up dominion over geographical regions. Their jurisdiction was given by God and empowered by the people in those lands (Daniel 10:20 NKJV). These are not natural political leaders but spiritual principalities influencing culture, government, and civil operations in their region.

Colossians 1:16 affirms that all things, including thrones, dominions, principalities, and powers, were created through Christ and for Him. If that is the case, then what are they and how do they function? How does understanding of their function and operation affect us today and what are we to do about them?

This chapter is not intended to be an exhaustive dive into this topic but rather to provoke deeper study. I would encourage you to take this to the Lord in your own personal study and devotional time. And dig a little deeper!

Where did it all start? Let's look in the book of Genesis.

God Divided the Nations

In Genesis 11, we read of the Tower of Babel and how God confused the language of the people and then separated and dispersed them. This dispersion led to the establishment of distinct nations or "ethnos" groups (from the Greek *ethnos,* meaning people, nation, or tribe) who share a common culture, language, and customs.

> When the Most High gave to the nations their inheritance, when he divided mankind, he fixed the borders of the peoples according to the number of the sons of God. But the Lord's portion is his people, Jacob his allotted heritage.
>
> —Deuteronomy 32:8-9 ESV

God separated the people at the Tower of Babel not only according to language but He gave them over to the "sons of God." God allowed the nations to follow after other gods or spiritual rulers in the heavenly realm. In fact, He—the one true God—allotted these lesser gods to have dominion over regions and ethnic groups of people. The spiritual control that these gods, or principalities, were given by God continue to operate even today. These spiritual principalities are at work to influence and control leaders and those in positions of influence around the world. They work like puppet masters to influence leaders, nations, and global events. They have spiritual "thrones" and they function from those thrones just as kings. A natural leader may rise and fall, but those principalities, or ancient thrones, continue to influence and even control regions, ethnic groups and world events.

While God allocated the nations to these gods, He reserved Israel for Himself. God was to be the King over Israel, and Israel was to be an example to the nations of what godly rulership would look like. Is it any wonder why there is such contention between Israel and the nations of the earth today?

It is significant that God so often warns the children of Israel not to follow other gods. Why would He need to warn them if the other gods were not a reality? Other gods are genuine entities and the temptation to follow after them remains real.

Other gods are genuine entities and the temptation to follow after them remains real.

Satan, or the devil, is referred to as "the god of this world," and he has corrupted those spirit beings. In fact, he has corrupted the whole earth. Both spiritual principalities and natural kingdoms have been corrupted by the devil.

God Has a Plan for the Nations

Although God separated the nations, He did not abandon them. Not at all. He always intended that all the nations of the earth would have the opportunity to seek after Him and find Him.

> And He made from one [common origin, one source, one blood] all nations of men to settle on the face of the earth, having definitely determined [their] allotted periods of time and the fixed boundaries of their habitation (their settlements, lands, and abodes), so that they should seek God, in the hope that they might feel after Him and find Him, although He is not far from each one of us.
>
> —Acts 17:26-27 AMPC

God determined when all these nations should rise and fall and decided their boundaries so that the nations might seek God, feel after Him and find Him. He is not far from any one of us.

In Mark 11:17, Jesus said that His temple would be called a house of prayer for all nations. God's desire was (and is) to include all peoples.

Though He separated the nations at Babel by language, in Acts 2 we see Him reunite them and He did it by language. Each person heard in their native language. The nations are also described as part of Christ's inheritance. In Psalm 2:8 (NKJV) declares, "Ask of Me, and I will give You the nations for Your inheritance." That promise shows how the nations are woven into God's redemptive plan, and how Jesus, as King of kings, will take His throne and rule over all the nations (Revelation 11:15).

God, because He is just, cannot violate His own word. The heavens belong to the Lord, but the earth is given into the hands of the sons of men (Psalm 115:16). By the permission of the people in a region, those principalities, with their thrones and dominion, still have been allowed the right to influence and govern the geographic region and people group of that region. For now, they maintain their ruling power by the consensus of the people, and they operate on lies to maintain that rule. Jesus, however, will return to judge the nations and reclaim them as His inheritance.

So, What Do We Do?

What are we to do in response to these "ancient thrones"? Do we simply accept it and say, "Well, it is what it is"? No! Jesus did something about these principalities and powers.

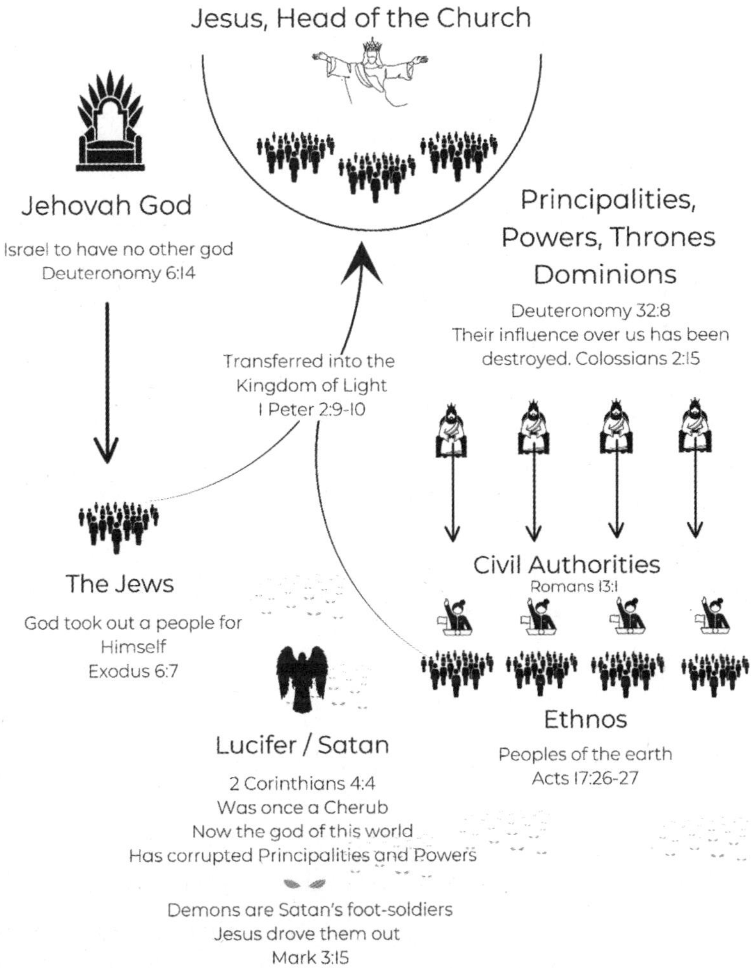
Jesus, Head of the Church
Jehovah God
Israel to have no other god
Deuteronomy 6:14
Principalities,
Powers, Thrones
Dominions
Deuteronomy 32:8
Their influence over us has been
destroyed. Colossians 2:15
Transferred into the
Kingdom of Light
I Peter 2:9-10
Civil Authorities
Romans 13:1
The Jews
God took out a people for
Himself
Exodus 6:7
Ethnos
Peoples of the earth
Acts 17:26-27
Lucifer / Satan
2 Corinthians 4:4
Was once a Cherub
Now the god of this world
Has corrupted Principalities and Powers
Demons are Satan's foot-soldiers
Jesus drove them out
Mark 3:15

These powers became corrupt and sought dominance over people and nations. Their influence depends on the level of submission from those within a region. Their power is not absolute but tied to the authority people grant them. Their authority *(exousia)* and influence *(thronos)* persist through collective agreement and submission of the people.

Jesus disarmed these powers, removing their legal right to dominate us. They now operate through deception, but Jesus, as Truth, has exposed their lies and given us light.

Our task isn't just to bind, lose, or declare, but it's to partner with God to influence people's choices toward righteousness and Jesus' authority. We can't simply command these powers to leave or try to dismantle their thrones. Their thrones are still legitimate and will remain until Jesus returns. He will judge the nations and their gods. They will "die like men" (Psalm 82:6-7).

Instead, we present Jesus as King and proclaim the gospel of His kingdom. When people enter God's kingdom, these principalities lose their influence, and God's reign and rule will expand.

Jesus gave us the key: preach the gospel, make disciples, care for others, and pray. As fewer people in the nations of the earth submit to these rulers, their power weakens, freeing individuals and transforming nations and cultures.

> Go then and make disciples of all the nations, baptizing them into the name of the Father and of the Son and of the Holy Spirit.
>
> —Matthew 28:19 NKJV

Jenny and I have both participated in missions trips into the Pacific Island nation of Fiji. Before the gospel came to those islands, they were a people of war, living in the mountains and even practicing cannibalism. After the gospel arrived, the culture was dramatically changed. The people moved out of the mountains to the coast and became peace-loving, welcoming, and so warm. It's now part of their culture! If you were ever to go there, you would be greeted with a heartfelt "bula," meaning "welcome."

We are to teach people of all ethnos groups. Immerse them. Baptize them in the name of Jesus, and help them and equip them with the Word of God. That will influence a nation or a region and take back that nation for God.

Colossians 2:14-15 explains that Christ canceled the record of charges against us, nailed it to the Cross, and disarmed the spiritual rulers and authorities, publicly shaming them. Thus, the spiritual rulers no longer hold legal power to keep us bound. We are free!

These spiritual rulers still hold on to some power to operate in the earth because Adam's race still holds authority in the earth until Jesus returns. Though we are now transferred out from the kingdom of darkness into the kingdom of light (Colossians 1:13), those principalities still try to exercise control and influence over the sons of disobedience (Ephesians 2:2).

Our Delegated Authority

As born-again believers, we are now children of God and have been given delegated authority, not absolute authority. Only Jesus holds absolute authority. Jesus disarmed principalities so they no longer rule over us. And He gave us spiritual weapons to resist them, but He didn't remove them entirely. These principalities still exist and influence worldly culture, government, and society.

Jesus will ultimately judge the nations; but for now, believers are to restrain these powers. We do this by leading people to salvation and operating prophetically, but only as directed by Jesus and the Holy Spirit. Exercising authority over principalities requires God's delegation; without it, we cannot act.

Exercising authority over principalities requires God's delegation; without it, we cannot act.

Sometimes, in prayer, we glimpse these powers and their influence. Our role is to report what we see to Jesus, listen for His instructions, and act only with His delegated authority, understanding the limits of our commission, as Paul did.

> We, on the other hand, will not boast beyond our legitimate province and proper limit, but will keep within the limits [of our commission which] God has allotted us as our measuring line and which reaches and includes even you.
>
> —2 Corinthians 10:13 AMPC

We must stay within our commission and not boast beyond our legitimate sphere. When He gives something to say, say it! And if you are faithful before God in prayer, He will give you something to say. It may not make a lot of sense to you, and you may feel like there should be more to say, but say what He says, just like Jeremiah did in Jeremiah chapter 1, and He will watch over His word to perform it.

Voice of the Prophet

More often than not, God will use the offices of the prophet and apostle to make inroads into the spiritual landscape of a nation.

I have a dear friend who is really invested in missions in a particular developing nation. While holding a prayer meeting there with some national pastors, she was given an assignment by God for that nation. There she saw, by discerning of spirits, a seat of governing authority. It was like a throne. She saw a great angel standing beside that seat and she listened for the Lord's instructions. They all prayed and released the angel to its place. Then she saw that angel sitting in that seat and she knew the job was done. She didn't bind the ruling, influencing principality or declare universal decrees; in fact, I don't believe she even saw that wicked principality. Instead, she obeyed exactly the Lord's direction in what to say. She commanded God's messenger to take that seat.

Afterward, there were tangible changes in that nation's government and it seemed the nation was opened to the gospel even more.

She explained it this way, "Exacting words and/or actions in how to address that and take authority.... It's not just shooting every shot you've got, quoting every scripture, binding and losing.... It's like getting a security code for a door and only that code will open it."

If we will listen to the voice of the Lord, listen for that "word" or code, report what He shows and say what He wants said, those principalities will be held back and God's plan for "all people to be saved" will advance.

Understanding how these principalities operate will change how we pray. When we see the truth, we will see that they operate on lies. When we realize the limits of their power, we will have great boldness to stand, using our delegated authority. When we have utterance, we speak out. We report to the Head what we see. This understanding will transform how we function in the kingdom of light

Yes, those principalities are still active; but we are not the ones to ultimately depose and eradicate them. That authority belongs to Jesus. Our mission is to lead people out of the influence of principalities, powers, thrones, and dominions into the freedom of Christ, and to pray, stand between those ruling powers and the people, and hold back their influence (Colossians 1:13). And say what we see in the spirit.

The Word of God gives us further insight into who our enemy is and how we can stand against and resist him.

What About Satan—the Devil?

Much could be said about the devil, or Satan, or the one who is our archenemy. We're not going to do a deep dive into this topic either but suffice it to say, he is our enemy and we no longer are held under his power, thanks to the redemptive work of Jesus.

The devil holds a kind of pre-eminence among all corrupt spirit beings, since he was the first to rebel and therefore became a "god" with a domain—the god of this world (2 Corinthians 4:4; Ephesians 2:2).

The devil's reign has corrupted the whole world, including those principalities and powers, thrones and dominions (1 John 5:19). In addition to that, he uses demons to afflict humans, especially believers.

The devil goes by many names that describe his function—devil, satan (meaning adversary or accuser), the wicked one, father of lies, Beelzebub, diabolos, and many more. According to Scripture, it is generally believed his name was Lucifer, which means "bearer of light" (2 Corinthians 11:14). He was part of the cherubim who ministered to God around the throne (Ezekiel 28:14). Because of his pride, he was cast down from heaven (Isaiah 14:12).

Satan is not omnipresent; he can be in only one place at a time and relies on demons to execute his plans, particularly to accuse, aggravate, and trouble the body of Christ.

What Jesus Said About the Devil

Jesus said: The devil is a murderer and the father of lies from the beginning (John 8:44). He is a thief who comes only to steal, kill, and destroy (John 10:10). Jesus resisted him and told him to leave (Matthew 4:1-10). He sows evil among believers (Matthew 13:25). He steals the Word (Matthew 13:18). He will try to sift you as he did with Peter (Luke 22:31).

Revelation 12:10 reveals that the accuser of the brethren, who accused them before God day and night, has been cast down. What Jesus did for us was to silence the accusations of the enemy.

The one thing we know for sure about Satan, or the devil, is that his power over us has been broken. Whatever the devil is trying to pull off as a prosecutor, he has no case against you. He is an accuser without any evidence.

What About Demons?

Demons don't get much mention in the Bible. They did, however, manifest in Jesus' earthly ministry as seen in the Gospels. They are low-class unclean spirits and Jesus showed us how to deal with them. He didn't hold discussion or debate; He treated demons like vermin. He simply commanded them to leave. Believers are instructed to "Resist the devil and he will flee from you" (James 4:7 NKJV).

A demon is a disembodied spirit looking for a body to occupy. That is the only way they are able to operate on earth. Because demons don't have a body to occupy, they are illegal aliens!

A principality or power doesn't require a human body. They hold positions in the spirit realm, and they operate from the spirit realm to influence whole groups of people and nations.

With demons, however, it's different. We can, just like Jesus did, cast out demons. While principalities war in regions and territories, demons war with humans.

During World War II, the Allied forces were fighting Nazi Germany. If you were to ask an Allied soldier who they were fighting, they would have said, "We are fighting Hitler!" Now I'm sure practically no Allied soldier ever saw Adolf Hitler. But in fighting the German troops, they were indirectly fighting the cause of Hitler. Similarly, more often than not, we are not directly dealing with Satan himself, but simply the demons who carry out his agenda.

Demons are just foot soldiers of the devil and all we need to do is resist them, simply tell them to leave and they must go.

The Weapons of our Warfare

We are engaged in warfare on two fronts. There are those bothersome demons that seek to trouble us like nuisance flies. And there are principalities and powers who seek to control us, our families, our city, and our nation.

There is a saying, "Fight fire with fire." That suggests the best way to overcome a challenge is to meet it head-on with equal or greater force of the same kind. However, the weapons we are given to fight with are far superior.

> For though we walk in the flesh, we do not war according to the flesh. For the weapons of our warfare are not carnal but mighty in God for pulling down strongholds, casting down arguments and every high thing that exalts itself against the knowledge of God, bringing every thought into captivity to the obedience of Christ.
>
> —2 Corinthians 10:3-5 NKJV

This passage reminds us that although we live in the flesh, our warfare is not with flesh, and human weapons are ineffective. The true battleground is in our own minds, where strongholds are built through thoughts and beliefs that are contrary to the knowledge of God and the truth. We must discover who we are in Christ. Knowing the truth about our identity will set us free from any attempt to control or manipulate us.

God has given us spiritual weapons powerful enough to pull down these strongholds, refute arguments and theories that oppose the truth, and bring every thought captive into Christ's obedience. In this we wrestle. It's a daily battle, but it's one we win!

> For we are not wrestling with flesh and blood [contending only with physical opponents], but against the despotisms, against the powers, against [the master spirits who are] the world rulers of this present darkness, against the spirit forces of wickedness in the heavenly (supernatural) sphere.
>
> —Ephesians 6:12 AMPC

Principalities and powers will attempt to exert their influence over nations, cities, churches, and even families, but you can stand firm in your God-given authority and resist the tide of evil in your own garden or sphere of influence.

Thank God for the weapons given to us. He has given us the name of Jesus, the Word of God, the anointing of the Holy Spirit with the gifts and fruit of the spirit. We apply the blood of Jesus by using our mouth and speaking. We also can use times of communion, remembering all Jesus has done for us, worshipping Him for that. Such amazing weapons! By utilizing and activating these weapons, we can overcome these strongholds and replace lies with the truth.

What God Says

> How dare the nations plan a rebellion. Their foolish plots are futile!
>
> Look at how the power brokers of the world rise up to hold their summit as the rulers scheme and confer together against YAHWEH and his Anointed King, saying:

"Let's come together and break away from the Creator. Once and for all let's cast off these controlling chains of God and his Christ!"

God-Enthroned merely laughs at them; the Sovereign One mocks their madness!

Then with the fierceness of his fiery anger, he settles the issue and terrifies them to death with these words:

"I myself have poured out my King on Zion, my holy mountain. I will reveal the eternal purpose of God. For he has decreed over me, 'You are my favored Son. And as your Father I have crowned you as my King Eternal. Today I became your Father. Ask me to give you the nations and I will do it, and they shall become your legacy. Your domain will stretch to the ends of the earth. And you will shepherd them with unlimited authority, crushing their rebellion as an iron rod smashes jars of clay!'

"Listen to me, all you rebel kings and all you upstart judges of the earth. Learn your lesson while there's still time. Serve and worship the awe-inspiring God. Recognize his greatness and bow before him, trembling with reverence in his presence. Fall facedown before him and kiss the Son before his anger is roused against you. Remember that his wrath can be quickly kindled! But many blessings are waiting for all who turn aside to hide themselves in him!"

—Psalm 2 TPT

PART THREE

ASPECTS OF GOD

As broad as the spirit realm is, the magnitude of God is even broader. He is infinite and has innumerable aspects of His person. Some of these aspects are what we may expect, like mercy and love. Some aspects could be considered to be the "dark side" of God, but we will discover even that side of God is glorious and worthy of worship.

7

THE MANY ASPECTS OF GOD

My God and I go in the fields together
We walk and talk as good friends should and do
We clasp our hands, our voices ring with laughter
My God and I walk through the meadow's hues
He tells me of the years that went before me
When heavenly plans were made for me to be
When all was but a dream of dim conceptions
To come to life earth's verdant glory see
My God and I will go for aye together
We'll walk and talk just as good friends do
This earth will pass and with it common trifles
But God and I will go unendingly
As I approach the portal high
Then shall the voice of the watchman cry
Enter O tired one, saved by grace
I shall look up and see His face
We'll clasp our hands our voices ring with laughter
My God and I will go unendingly.
"My God and I" by I.B. Sergei (aka Austris Wihtol), 1935

Knowing God

There is a reality of clasping God's hand. In places that are unfamiliar, His hand is familiar. It really doesn't matter where He leads you as long as you can feel that familiar hand. When you really know God, life does not have to be just commonplace; indeed it never will be. He lets you live by faith, and things are always new and wonderful in Him. To know God is a lifelong pursuit and more because to know all there is of God will not only take our whole life, it will take all of eternity.

There are always new and wonderful aspects of God. He never ceases to thrill me, and the wonders of His person are so beautiful. There are parts of God that I have become very familiar with, but there is actually more to see and know about God, and in the seeing and knowing of it, we can operate in it.

When you come to know more about Him, what was once unfamiliar becomes so much a part of Him that it is familiar. Your love of Him grows, and your understanding of Him is wider and fuller. Even the parts of God that may have seemed a contradiction to what you love about Him become more and more familiar as you come to know Him more.

Actually what seems like the "dark side" of God is very light. There is no dark side of God because God is light. I know that in the God I love there is nothing that is unlovely. He is altogether lovely; He is absolutely brilliant.

God is altogether lovely and He is light. There is never any part of God that we should draw back from. If part of Him is unfamiliar to us, we could find ourselves tempted to draw back from that, even though it is part of God Himself. Some of us may have drawn back from the baptism of the Holy Spirit or maybe a move of the Spirit that seemed unfamiliar to us. But when we begin to see that part of God in the light of who He is, that part is no longer unfamiliar to us. In fact, we find ourselves desiring to know more about that part of God.

There is never any part of God that we should draw back from.

A Dark Side of God?

There is part of God that many draw back from because it does seem "dark." However, in the light of the Word and in the light that the Holy Spirit is so capable of revealing and enlightening our spirits with, everything is beautiful. That part of God people could draw back from, actually in the light of revelation, you find yourself in cadence with and in expectancy of. You find that part of God becomes more familiar, and it is consistent with His nature and what you already know about Him.

God could not reveal all of Himself at one time. He revealed parts of Himself in His names so people would know who He is and how to respond to Him. There are the Jehovah Names: Jehovah Nissi, Jehovah Jireh, Jehovah Rapha, and so on. He never revealed all of Himself all on one day; He couldn't. It was not that He wasn't able; we are not able to receive all of Him in one day.

Many times, the seasons of our life and the seasons of time itself give a platform on which God can reveal Himself. You cannot push some of these things; you cannot sit and theologically learn some of these things. Life has to give you the opportunity to walk hand in hand with God. And in walking with Him, hand in hand, parts of Him become more apparent.

I look forward to every year of life. I don't fear to grow older; I yearn for what life gives me the opportunity to know that I could never know any other way. I may know it by precept, but the experience of God can only be experienced in measure! So bring on the years and bring on more of God! I am so glad that this life could not contain all of what we will know of God. We are going to walk with Him for all of eternity!

> Light is sown for the righteous, and gladness for the upright in heart.
>
> —Psalm 97:11 NKJV

Has God ever disappointed you with Himself? He is not disappointing. He is fascinating. God appeals to something in the human spirit

God appeals to something in the human spirit that is way beyond curiosity.

that is way beyond curiosity. It may begin in curiosity, but it opens up a place in your spirit that makes you insatiable for anything else. You want to learn more about Him and know more of Him. So even the parts of Him that are unfamiliar become familiar to you, and you grow to love that part of Him and love Him more for it. God reveals Himself portion by portion, piece by piece.

Have you ever worked on a jigsaw puzzle? I like to work on puzzles. You can just dive in and try to get the frame and some identifiable object within the picture, but every day you walk past that table, you look and you find another piece, another section. And you put a little more together, adding to the bigger picture. Then a piece that didn't fit for the longest time suddenly fits! You find a piece over here and there and join them together, and then you find a good portion of the picture, but it's not the whole picture. Then you find a piece that joins whole portions together. It gives you this sense of precious delight! It's wonderful!

Coming to know God is a bit like that. You see a piece of Him that seems not to fit, but as you look at Him every day, gradually the bits come together, and you find yourself knowing Him a little more every day.

God of Justice and Judgment

We know God is love. That's the part of God we first come to know when we are born again. We love that about Him and worship Him for that. As we look more into His person, we discover more about Him. He is also the God of justice and judgment. We may never discover the whole picture of this part of God, but as you read the Bible, your spirit will be sensitized to this particular puzzle. You will see verses that you have read but never really saw before. Your eyes will see them and your spirit will be excited!

In the days and years to come, the Holy Spirit will give revelation through the gifts, and many different ways and more pieces will be added to the picture.

If you are looking for complete understanding of this part of God, then look to Him because He is the completed picture. In Him is the truth, and the truth gives you light in which to work in prayer; so when He asks you to do something, you won't draw back from doing it because you don't know the truth.

> I could ask the darkness to hide me and the light around me to become night—but even in darkness I cannot hide from you. To you the night shines as bright as day. Darkness and light are the same to you.
>
> —Psalm 139:11-12 NLT

To Know Him More

One of my life's pursuits has been to know God more. Ever since I was a young teenager and saw the obvious presence of God on some of the older people in my dad's church, I was determined to know God in the same manner they did.

Then there was a really dramatic time in my life, back in 1977, when I had an encounter with the Lord. I came really close to Him and desired to know Him just as Paul had written in Philippians 3:

> [For my determined purpose is] that I may know Him [that I may progressively become more deeply and intimately acquainted with Him, perceiving and recognizing and understanding the wonders of His Person more strongly and more clearly], and that I may in that same way come to know the power outflowing from His resurrection [which it exerts over believers], and that I may so share His sufferings as to be continually transformed [in spirit into His likeness even] to His death, [in the hope].
>
> —Philippians 3:10 AMPC

That has become my life's pursuit. And all through my life, whatever I have seen about Him, He has never been a disappointment to me. On the contrary, every part of Him is lovely, even the parts of His person that may seem dark.

There are so many aspects of God that we are yet to discover. The Holy Spirit's ministry to us is to guide us into all truth. In fact, we are told in Scripture that the Holy Spirit "searches diligently, exploring *and* examining everything, even sounding the profound and bottomless things of God" (1 Corinthians 2:10 AMPC). So even the dark, bottomless, and seemingly unknowable parts of God are worth seeking out by the ministry of the Holy Spirit.

Let us lean into the depths of God and love everything we see about Him. There is much that we are able to see and sound out on this side of eternity. Things that may seem more like the dark side of God actually turn out to be all part of His divine nature, His divine plan, and the very essence of God—Love itself.

8

THE JUDGMENTS OF GOD

Righteousness and justice are the foundation of Your throne; mercy and loving-kindness and truth go before Your face.

—Psalm 89:14 AMPC

The Nature of God

God is love. Love is not simply an action He performs. It is the essence of His very being. He cannot cease to be love, no matter what we do; if He did, He would no longer be God. There's nothing you can do to ever get Him to quit loving you because He'd have to quit being God. Some people think that what they did was so especially bad that He surely would quit loving them. You're not that amazing! You can't make God quit being God just because of something you did wrong over and over and over again. No! God's love is unwavering.

The Hebrew word for *love* is *ahava* and means "to give." Love, by its nature, seeks to give rather than receive. Love is a core attribute of God. But love isn't the only thing about God. He's also holy; He is also righteous. He is just and He is judge. He is all this in every age and dispensation. Why? Because He cannot change.

The aspects of God are so wide we couldn't possibly take them all in at one time. But in different seasons and generations, different elements of God's nature are emphasized and brought into the light.

Sometimes, the body of Christ really needs a certain message like faith or love, so God shines a spotlight on it for a while. It's not that everything else becomes redundant; it's just that we need a boost in that area, like a concentrated vitamin or hormone. The goal is always a healthy, balanced Church. We need all of God's truth because Jesus is Truth itself.

The Righteous Judge

> "But let him who glories glory in this, that he understands and knows Me, that I am the Lord, exercising lovingkindness, judgment, and righteousness in the earth, for in these I delight," says the Lord.
>
> —Jeremiah 9:24 NKJV

There are a few characteristics of God in this verse. First, there is *lovingkindness.* We know that He wants to exercise this in the earth; God wants to demonstrate His lovingkindness and how it can be ministered to people. Then there's His *righteousness,* His holiness. This is how we've come to know Him, and we are delighted in this. Aren't you thankful that not only is He righteous, but He's made you righteous? Praise the name of the Lord!

But I'd like us to look at a specific aspect of God. This verse says, "I am the Lord, exercising... judgment...in the earth, for in these I delight." So, we know that He delights in lovingkindness; we know that He delights in righteousness, but let's look at how He delights in judgment. Wow, really? Judgment can be a very scary word—a word that has put many people "off" regarding God.

When it is not connected to God, not within truth, and not delivered in a way that is in line with His Word, the word *judgment* has brought condemnation and shame to people and has actually driven them away from God.

God being the Righteous Judge is something that has made people angry at Him. Isn't that a weird thing? But it is so. I remember when the Lord was dealing with me some years ago about judgment, and I did some study on it. I had the realization that this part of God isn't one that I necessarily worship. When we worship Him, we worship His goodness, His kindness and healing, and that He provides all these wonderful things. But we don't often worship Him saying, "Oh, thank You, You're such a good judge."

But I'll never forget what the Lord told me. He said, "If you don't love the judgment part of Me, or the part of Me that is Judge, it's simply because you do not know that part of Me correctly." He said, "If you knew it in truth, you would love it."

There is no dark side to God. So the judgment side of God is not the dark side of the force; it's not the Jekyll part of God, the part that no one wants to see. No, the judgment side of God is altogether wonderful, and so we're going to see how in the world that can be.

The Age of Grace

When Jesus was in the temple, He opened to this scripture in Isaiah 61 and He read it:

> The Spirit of the Lord is upon Me, because He has anointed Me to preach the gospel to the poor; He has sent Me to heal the brokenhearted, to proclaim liberty to the captives and recovery of sight to the blind, to set at liberty those who are oppressed; to proclaim the acceptable year of the Lord.
>
> —Luke 4:18-19 NKJV

Jesus read as far as verse 19 and He closed the book! Isaiah 61 had more, but Jesus closed the book at verse 19! It was right that He closed the book because Jesus was introducing a brand-new age, a brand-new dispensation. He closed the book on one dispensation and opened the book on another.

The ministry of Jesus is full of grace and truth. He introduced the possibility that the God they knew as God the Creator and God the Judge could also be God the Father. No one had ever called Him such a name before, but Jesus called Him "God, My Father."

Jesus closed the book after He read "to proclaim the acceptable year of the Lord" and before the words "the day of vengeance of our God." Does that mean there is still to come a day of vengeance of our God? Decidedly, YES! Absolutely! The Bible refers to it as the Great Day of the Lord and there is a great day coming. But Jesus in that particular time didn't make reference to God in the Day of Vengeance. He wanted to bring light to the "acceptable year of the Lord," the Year of Jubilee, the day of acceptance with God, the day when our captivity is ended.

Aren't you glad we are living in the year of Jubilee!

It still doesn't do away with the fact that there is a day of vengeance with our God. Jesus opened the way for mercy, but He did not do away with judgment.

In the current dispensation, the age of grace, God's love is emphasized through the gift of His Son, Jesus. Jesus highlighted love over judgment, instructing us not to judge others. This does not mean other aspects of God's character, such as justice, are negated; rather, they may simply not be as prominent in this time.

Jesus opened the way for mercy, but He did not do away with judgment.

There was something about the mercy of God that was so highlighted at the Cross that it greatly impacted the dispensation we are in right now. God really wants to emphasize His love and mercy for the world, and it may appear that He has pulled back a little on judgment. So, if God is not sending fire and brimstone, or opening cavernous rifts in the earth to swallow up the wicked, how is justice to be served? God is still the just God and there is sure a great need for justice to be made available for the weak, the oppressed, and the vulnerable.

The Judgments of God in the Church

Judgment as seen meted out in the Old Testament makes some people squirm and become uncomfortable. But actually, the more you come to know God the less uncomfortable you are with the fact that God is the Judge. It gives you a "safe" feeling. It would make you feel uncomfortable if you felt that He was a judge like the worldly judges among us, but our God is the Righteous Judge. It is very comforting to know that He is "just" and the scepter of His kingdom is a scepter of righteousness. The symbol of His throne and of His kingdom is righteousness. That has never been perverted. His scepter, or symbol of authority, has never been bent. It is a straight scepter (Hebrews 1:8-9 NKJV).

This wonderful revelation that Jesus introduced us to, this dispensation of grace in which we live, is in the very last portions of time, like the last grains of sand in the hourglass. Another age and time are about to begin. But during this dispensation of grace, did God cease to be Judge? Is this dispensation of grace just a "whoop-de-do" time when everybody can get away with, literally, murder? It appears that they think that God winks at anything! It seems that sinners think they can buy Him off; the Church thinks they can buy Him off! But God will not be bought off by anyone!

Continuing Judgments

Judgments did not cease during this dispensation—not if the Scripture is true, and it is. They are not things that we meditate very much upon, and we don't really speak too much about them, but nonetheless they are there in God's Word, the Bible.

For example, in Acts 5:1-10 Ananias and Sapphira lied to the Holy Ghost and they died for it—in church! The Bible says that the people feared and they were very careful about joining themselves to that church!

Then in Acts 12, there was a king by the name of Herod who thought he was God. He was full of himself—but then he was full of worms. The Bible says the angel of the Lord struck him! In Acts 12:7 the angel of the Lord delivered Peter out of prison, and then in verse 23 that same angel struck King Herod with worms and King Herod died. This is in the church age in the book of Acts, freshly after the Holy Ghost had been poured out.

The Vengeance of God

> Beloved, never avenge yourselves, but leave the way open for [God's] wrath; for it is written, Vengeance is Mine, I will repay (requite), says the Lord.
>
> —Romans 12:19 AMPC

Vengeance belongs to God, so we are to leave the way open for God to avenge. He will avenge the right of a person who has been abused or treated wrongly.

Have you ever had a surge of adrenalin come into your flesh, wanting to defend or even avenge someone who has been wronged? I have. I have visually pictured myself, coming to the defense of a child who was abused. It gave me a sense of strange pleasure and satisfaction to think that I could just take someone by the hair and kick 'em with my knee! I've never had that urge for the defense of myself, but I have had that for the defense of children.

Vengeance belongs to God, so we are to leave the way open for God to avenge.

Here's an amazing truth! According to Romans 12:19, we could actually block His vengeance if we get involved in meting out retribution. This scripture also says that God's vengeance is still available in this dispensation!

The Escalation of Judgments on Earth

There is something very interesting that we need to see from this standpoint. In Deuteronomy chapter 7 after God brought His people out of Egypt, He told them to not be afraid and also to remember what He did in Egypt. This was to be a huge monument for them. The Passover was to be a point of reference every year for them, not just the blood on the doorpost and eating the lamb in haste. They were to remember the whole story of Egypt and the exodus.

This should cause you to think and wonder why Egypt was so important? Why would God use this as a point of reference? Egypt is where God manifested His great delivering power, and He did it through judgments. That is not to be despised; that is to be investigated.

The judgments of God were not directed at the people. They were directed against the Egyptian gods, and the people felt the force of these judgments. God was in effect saying, "You gods think you're so mighty, holding My people captive. I'll show you I still have power over you all!" And so, God judged the gods—and, by extension, the Pharaoh and also people. Each of the plagues targeted a specific god and aspect of Egyptian culture and belief. For example, the first plague of water turning to blood targeted the Nile gods and the plague of darkness was a direct assault on the sun god Ra. The final plague of the death of the firstborn struck at the divine status of the Pharaoh himself.

In this we can learn something about God's nature and the way judgments come. Judgments *escalate*. They don't start with the worst. In this way God showed His mercy. Judgments start with the least. They give people an opportunity to repent, and they give people a choice.

It would be as if you were driving on a road that ended in a bridge that had collapsed. There would be a sign posted far in advance. The closer you got, the more signs would be set up. There would be barricades and bigger barricades. If you went by all those warning signs, then have it your way, but you were warned! Your car falls into a deep ravine.

The plagues in Egypt were like that. They started out pretty simple. The last judgment was very personal—the slaying of the firstborn. In meting out judgments in the Old Testament, God also used armies.

> Thus says the Lord to His anointed, To Cyrus, whose right hand I have held—to subdue nations before him and loose the armor of kings, to open before him the double doors, so that the gates will not be shut.
>
> —Isaiah 45:1 NKJV

This is just one example. In the Old Testament, there are many other examples where God used armies to mete out judgments.

Another way judgment is served is when there is an escalation of sin, of evil and iniquity. When sin abounds in the land and the volume of sin increases until the land itself can no longer contain the sin, the inhabitants of the land will be spit out.

Leviticus 18:25-30 talks about the sins of the nations that were dispossessed by the Israelites in the Promised Land. There is a limit to which the land can hold this volume of sin. There is some type of connection between the people who live on the earth and the earth being able to tolerate the people who live upon it. We were made from the earth and came from the dust of the earth. We see this connection with the blood of Abel that cried out from the ground after he was murdered (Genesis 4:10).

In Leviticus 18 it says that the ground will spit them out. It won't spit them out in a week, but there comes a time when the iniquity, the perversion and the atrocities that are done against innocent people, fill up the land, and the land will spit them out.

This is not a beautiful picture, but in this we can see something beautiful about the nature of God. He is not looking for every opportunity to slap people down and hurt them. God gets our attention gradually and gives every opportunity for us to repent. He did it through judgments, and He still does it through judgments.

Coming Judgments

There are divine judgments yet to be meted out in the Church. We may not have believed it, but Scripture supports that it does happen, even in this dispensation of grace. We will see it more in times to come. The more the glory is in operation, the more we will see these kinds of judgments.

Revelation 20 talks about a Great White Throne judgment. If you are at the Great White Throne judgment, it means that you have rejected the only way of salvation and you will be eternally damned and separated from God. That's HUGE! That's at the end of the escalation.

Judgment for the Body of Christ

For the body of Christ, there is also a day of reckoning. Romans 14:10 and 2 Corinthians 5:10 speak of the judgment seat of Christ. Every one of us will give an account of what we have done in our life, not how good our heart was.

You may ask, "What if I ask God to forgive me?" It is clear that you are forgiven and that sin is separated from you as far as the east is from the west. But what if all you did in life were things you had to ask God to forgive? Those things you had to ask forgiveness for are separated from you because of the blood of Jesus and the forgiveness that Jesus has provided for us. But all your works are not separated from you. These works will go with you to the judgment seat of Christ.

The Greek word used here for the word *judgment* is *bema.* The bema was a raised platform where Olympic judges awarded crowns to the victors. The judgment seat of Christ is not about condemnation but commendation. It's a review of your faithfulness and obedience to God.

When Jesus said, "It is finished," He meant the penalty of sin was fully paid. Therefore, believers are not judged for sin. We are judged for service in the same way an athlete is judged for their performance.

> So now there is no condemnation for those who belong to Christ Jesus.
>
> —Romans 8:1 NLT

Works done without God's leading, our "wood, hay, and stubble," will burn away, no matter how good they seemed at the time. Only what was directed by God and done in obedience, our "gold, silver, and precious stones," will follow us into eternity (1 Corinthians 3:12-13). Some will enter eternity with very little to show for their life's work, yet they themselves will still be saved "as through fire" (1 Corinthians 3:15 NKJV).

I think that would be most horrible! Brother Hagin pointed that out to me. Because of having looked into the face of Jesus before and knowing that one day he will stand before Him, he said that every day of his life he thought about standing before Jesus and giving an account of his life. Because of the reality I saw in his eyes, it made me think about it too. It becomes a strong motivation to consider how you live today in light of that day.

We can clearly see that there are coming judgments for the world and the Church at the end of time. We have also seen that there are escalating judgments in the earth. God is the absolute Judge, but He is also the God who desires justice in the earth and has always desired justice, not only at the end, but here and now for those who are living in the earth.

In this dispensation, when the judgments of God are withheld to a great degree, how is justice served? Does God just let everyone get away with injustice, unrighteousness, and the outworking of sin? No, He still cares about justice and has established another channel that He uses in dispensing justice in our dispensation.

9

THE JUSTICE OF GOD

The Lord is King forever and ever;
The nations have perished out of His land.
Lord, You have heard the desire of the humble;
You will prepare their heart;
You will cause Your ear to hear,
To do justice to the fatherless and the oppressed,
That the man of the earth may oppress no more.

—Psalm 10:16-18 NKJV

Justice in this Dispensation

In this dispensation or the church age or the age of grace, we see the judgment of God on the earth held back in great measure. The church age is when the mercy of God is wide open for all to be saved. God is giving every human on the earth the opportunity to seek after Him and find Him.

Even though the grace of God is highlighted and the mercy of God is openly on offer, the justice of God is as significantly important. People cry out for justice, and justice must be carried out for the sake of the vulnerable and the oppressed.

> So that men will say, "Surely there is a reward for the righteous; surely He is God who judges in the earth."
>
> —Psalm 58:11 NKJV

The psalmist declares that people must be able to recognize there is the God who rewards the righteous and judges the earth. Justice demonstrates God's lovingkindness by fixing things that are rough, making them smooth, and making crooked things straight. Justice demonstrates God's faithfulness by correcting wrongs and revealing what is true and fair, while injustice can cause doubt about God's goodness and lovingkindness.

> Yes, in the path of Your judgments, O Lord, we wait [expectantly] for You; our heartfelt desire is for Your name and for the remembrance of You. My soul yearns for You [O Lord] in the night, yes, my spirit within me seeks You earnestly; for [only] when Your judgments are in the earth will the inhabitants of the world learn righteousness (uprightness and right standing with God).
>
> —Isaiah 26:8-9 AMPC

This passage is a prayer of longing for God's judgment. Only then will the inhabitants of the earth learn righteousness. This isn't the righteousness of God that we have in Christ Jesus but the practical rightness that comes from His justice being dispensed. In this era, the Church can and should pray for God's justice to be unveiled, trusting that through prayer, entire groups and even societies can be transformed. We pray for straightening what is crooked and preparing the way for the Lord's return.

God's Plan for Civil Authorities

God desires justice! But how is justice delivered? God still cares about justice, and judgments still need to be made for the sake of righteousness. God has set in place a system of authority to deliver justice and judgment for the people.

God has established civic authorities to administer judgment and justice on earth. According to 1 Peter 2 and Romans 13, those in authority are appointed as God's ministers, regardless of who they are personally. There are seats for people to sit in, which are seats that have been established by God. These are seats of authority. The people who sit in those seats have a job to uphold justice, punishing evil and praising those who do right.

God has set in place a system of authority to deliver justice and judgment for the people.

From God's perspective, the seat of authority itself is ordained by Him. It is not merely an office of the state or the nation. It is not the person individually. It is the position that carries the authority.

A striking example of the impact of righteous authority can be seen in Singapore. Tony and I, with our two girls, Liliana and Annalisa, lived there for four years in the early 2000s. It may be different now, but this is what it was like when we lived there.

After breaking away from Malaysia, Singapore faced poverty and external threats. It was a very small island that was mainly mosquito-ridden and had very little prospect of prosperity. Its leaders identified corrupting influences such as prostitution, drugs, gangs, and gambling and outlawed them with strict penalties. In just over a decade, Singapore rose from poverty to first-world status, to a nation that was renowned for its safety and discipline.

The environment was so secure that even young children could travel alone without fear. We could put our two young daughters in a taxi and send them to church or to school with absolutely no second thoughts! I'm in no way saying all nations need to imitate Singapore's model, but this example demonstrated to us how upholding justice can transform society.

The passages in 1 Peter 2:13 and Romans 13 teach that civil authorities are appointed by God to maintain justice and order in the civil arena:

> For the Lord's sake, submit to all human authority—whether the king as head of state, or the officials he has appointed. For

> the king has sent them to punish those who do wrong and to honor those who do right.
>
> —1 Peter 2:13-14 NLT

> Let every soul be subject to the governing authorities. For there is no authority except from God, and the authorities that exist are appointed by God. Therefore whoever resists the authority resists the ordinance of God, and those who resist will bring judgment on themselves. For rulers are not a terror to good works, but to evil. Do you want to be unafraid of the authority? Do what is good, and you will have praise from the same. For he is God's minister to you for good. But if you do evil, be afraid; for he does not bear the sword in vain; for he is God's minister, an avenger to execute wrath on him who practices evil. Therefore you must be subject, not only because of wrath but also for conscience' sake. For because of this you also pay taxes, for they are God's ministers attending continually to this very thing. Render therefore to all their due: taxes to whom taxes are due, customs to whom customs, fear to whom fear, honor to whom honor.
>
> —Romans 13:1-7 NKJV

Notice that three times in the Romans 13 passage, Paul calls these civil authorities "ministers." They are God's ministers. They are not preaching from a pulpit and may not even be Christian, but from the seat of authority they occupy, they are God's ministers. They work on God's behalf.

God's Ministers in Civic Arenas

We are familiar with "ministers" in church, but this is in the civil arena. People who are in authority, in those positions of authority, are God's ministers. In Commonwealth nations such as Australia where we live, those elected to parliament are actually called "ministers."

In most nations they are called public servants or servants of the people, or they are employees of the state or the nation. But from God's point of view, who set up the seats of authority in the first place, they don't just belong to their nation, they belong to God. They may be an employee of the nation, but according to Romans 13, they are a minister of God.

Well, what if they're not saved? It doesn't matter if they're not saved because they are not in that seat of authority to minister healing, love, mercy, and kindness. They're not in that seat of authority to minister the truth of the word of God. They are in that place of authority to minister justice and punishment for those who do wrong and to acknowledge those who are doing good.

The person in a seat of authority is God's minister and avenger to execute judgment.

The person in a seat of authority is God's minister and avenger to execute judgment. They are God's "avengers"! That's such strong language! The New King James Bible version says, "...for he is God's minister, an avenger to *execute* wrath on him who practices evil" (Romans 13:4). That word *execute* in the Greek is *ekdikos,* one whose role is to punish in order to carry out justice. And they do it as God's ministers, attending continually to this very thing.

Paul also goes on to say you must be subject to them not only because you fear wrath and their punishment, but also for the sake of your own conscience (Romans 13:5).

It is crucial to recognize the significance of those who serve in civil authority as God's ministers. Pastors, as God's ministers, need God's help and grace to lead congregations. In the same way judges, officials, and those in authority need divine wisdom and assistance to administer justice righteously. Without this grace or anointing, justice becomes twisted and perverted, and when judgment is not served properly, it reflects poorly on God's nature. Civic authority is meant to display God's justice, just as the Church is called to manifest His goodness and mercy. The one needs the other.

> Righteousness and justice are the foundation of Your throne; mercy and truth go before Your face.
>
> —Psalm 89:14 NKJV

When justice is not seen, people may doubt God's goodness or even existence, asking, "If there is a God, why do bad things happen?" But when justice is truly revealed, it points people to God, demonstrating that He is present and active, and His mercy is available.

Civil authorities have been established by God to keep people from doing the wrong thing and to encourage good behavior. If you do what's right, there's no need to worry about those in charge. They're supposed to look out for people who do the right thing. Authorities are there for our benefit, keeping things safe and fair. Sure there are times when some might mess up or not protect people as they should, but at the core of their God-given function, authorities are there to help society run smoothly.

Their job is to make sure justice is done, not just to let things slide. They are there to enforce the rules fairly. And they need God's wisdom, grace, and anointing to carry out their job.

The Authority Is in the Seat

The authority for civil authorities to function comes from the seat they are sitting in, not from whether they are good people or not, or even whether they are Christian or not. There are many examples in the Bible of how God used those sitting in seats of authority for His purposes. Some of them were good kings, like King David (Acts 13:22,36). Some were unrighteous, but God still used them, like King Cyrus (Isaiah 44:28; 45:1-3). Some were straight-out evil, like Pharaoh, but God said, "For this very purpose I have raised you up, that I may show My power in you, and that My name may be declared in all the earth" (Romans 9:17 NKJV).

Christians are called to submit to these authorities and pray for justice to be delivered. When we pray for justice, we activate these authorities to perform their God-given roles.

A Dream

Many years ago I had a dream that lasted all night long. It was a horrible dream. In that dream I saw humans torturing humans. I'd wake myself up, and I'd try to change it, but it wouldn't go away. I'd go back to sleep, and that dream would still be there.

The next night I went to sleep, and that dream came back, and I woke up. I thought, *I'm not going to have one more night with this dream.* Then it dawned on me! *I wonder if the Lord's trying to help me see something here.* So I said, "Father, are You trying to show me something in this dream?" As soon as I said that, I saw something. I had a vision of a massive room, and it was full of human suffering inflicted by other humans. There were children, too. Well, it became too much to bear. I cried out, "Lord, do something!" He said, "I'm doing the most I can with the prayer I'm getting."

At that moment the scene shifted, and that whole massive room where there was all that suffering became a chamber in God's heart. And at that moment, I loved Him more than I had ever known I could love Him because I knew that He was touched with the pain of people who are suffering. What stayed with me from that dream was what the Lord said to me, "I'm doing the most I can with the prayer I'm getting."

Does God Really Care?

It's a sad fact that many people struggle to believe in God because of the perception that He doesn't care about human suffering, that He doesn't care about their personal suffering. God cares about human suffering, and He cares enough to provoke us to do something about it.

Remember, God needs our voice in the earth to activate His promises and His power. He needs our prayer in order to move in the earth. And in this age of grace, when the mercy of God is highlighted, His justice is still needed, especially for the weak and the vulnerable. Some situations may need mercy, but crooked things need justice.

We are to cry out for justice. While mercy is necessary for those who have sinned, there are situations that specifically demand justice.

Crooked and unjust circumstances need to be straightened, and this is part of preparing the way for the coming of the Lord.

The Bible has much to say about orphans and widows, the poor and the needy. Solomon prayed for wisdom to work justice regarding these groups of people. Because their voices are muffled and gagged, somebody has to lift up a voice for them. There are people crying out and no one is hearing them. The Holy Spirit will help us to hear them so we can lift up our voice and ask God for justice for them.

> Woe to those who decree unrighteous decrees, who write misfortune, which they have prescribed to rob the needy of justice, and to take what is right from the poor of My people, that widows may be their prey, and that they may rob the fatherless.
>
> —Isaiah 10:1-2 NKJV

> He will bring justice to the poor of the people; He will save the children of the needy, and will break in pieces the oppressor.
>
> —Psalm 72:4 NKJV

> I know that the Lord will maintain the cause of the afflicted, and justice for the poor.
>
> —Psalm 140:12 NKJV

The Church Is Not the Dispenser of Justice

According to the Scripture, the authorized dispenser of justice in this dispensation is not the Church. It's not our role. While Christians are often involved in acts that help others, such as providing food, clothing, and medicine, these acts are more closely associated with mercy. Some Christians are also called as missionaries, to be involved in arenas that deliver justice, like law enforcement, politics, and justice groups.

God has strong words against injustice, and He acts to break the power of oppressors. However, when the body of Christ tries to deliver justice, it comes off as "judgmental." That's just not our role.

In all this, the Church isn't meant to be the group handing out justice. The Church is called to show compassion, kindness, and healing, just like Jesus did. Our job is to be generous and merciful, including praying for people who've done wrong. When Jesus was here, He focused on helping and showing mercy, not on punishing people.

Ultimate judgment and justice will come later, when Jesus comes to judge the nations of the earth. But for now, the Church is all about mercy and helping people break free from what holds them back. We're not fighting against people—our battle is spiritual. Still, justice is always close to God's heart, even now.

The Importance of Praying for Justice

Law enforcement and the justice system face many challenges, including the temptation for corruption. Our prayers can help support and strengthen them, ensuring justice is carried out. The justice system is an agency of God and should not be discarded because of its flaws; instead, we should pray for its integrity and effectiveness.

Your prayers don't just activate Christians. Your prayers activate God's ministers of justice, which may be saved or maybe not. But they are still ministers of God, not for mercy or the love of God, but for justice. Those who are in law enforcement, those in courts of law, those who are politicians and in the public sector, they are not to be left stranded! They are to be helped by God, and they are helped by God through our prayers.

Aligning Our Thoughts with God's Purposes

As we continue to move in the flow of God's purposes, we may need to adjust our thinking to align with His Word rather than our own opinions or the prevailing views of the world. God may use the most unexpected people in seats of authority to bring about His plan to deliver justice and even judgment where it is needed.

They need wisdom! If they don't get wisdom from above, they will default to the wisdom that comes from below.

> This wisdom does not descend from above, but is earthly, sensual, demonic. For where envy and self-seeking exist, confusion and every evil thing are there. But the wisdom that is from above is first pure, then peaceable, gentle, willing to yield, full of mercy and good fruits, without partiality and without hypocrisy.
>
> —James 3:15-17 NKJV

From our position seated with Christ, we can see things from God's perspective and gain a wide panorama of the plan of God. Our motivation to pray is by the unction of the Holy Spirit, not according to our own assessment of the situation.

We use this high place in Christ to work together with God so that the will of God can be accomplished on earth. When the righteous are in authority, the people rejoice (Proverbs 29:2 NKJV). Of course we want righteous leaders, but if we are the righteous in Christ Jesus, we need to take up our authority.

Scripture highlights the need for prayer in this area. Isaiah 59:4 (NKJV) laments that "no one calls out for justice, nor does any plead for truth." Through prayer, the Church can appeal for God's justice to be manifest in the earth. Psalm 58:11 (NKJV) declares, "Surely there is a reward for the righteous; surely He is God who judges in the earth." True justice—when wrongs are made right and the crooked is made straight—reveals God's hand in the world.

> When the righteous are in authority, the people rejoice; but when a wicked man rules, the people groan.
>
> —Proverbs 29:2 NKJV

We can partner with God to bring about justice, mercy, and the fulfilment of His plans on earth. Let us be willing vessels, allowing God to use us for His purposes through persistent and faith-filled prayer.

Let us pray for those in authority for God's justice to be executed in order for His lovingkindness to be revealed to the world. In doing so, we help pave the way for God's purposes to be fulfilled on earth.

10

THE MERCY OF GOD

Prayer is such a privilege; it didn't come without cost. Our privilege of being able to approach God anytime, and actually at His definition to come—and His invitation to come, actually even boldly—that did not come without cost to Him, great cost, great cost. It cost Him the life of His Son; it cost His Son His blood. Thank You, Lord Jesus, that He gave and poured all of it on our behalf to reconcile us.

—Patsy Cameneti, 2018

Perspective and Assignment

One of the most amazing things about our seating of authority given to us in Christ Jesus is that not only can we operate with that authority, but it also gives us a much higher perspective. We actually are able to see things the way God sees them. We are able to tap into the mind of God and look at the world through His eyes. That gives us a tremendous advantage in that we are able to see things from the beginning to the end. We can see the plans of God, and we can see with His love and compassion. He will use our eyes to see things on the earth from His perspective.

One of the ways we can see from His perspective is to understand the nature of sin and God's heart to bring restoration. God judged all sin in Jesus. Jesus was tortured, beaten, went through His passion in the Garden of Gethsemane, was taken to Pilate's hall, and eventually was nailed to the Cross. He had His side pierced, He died, and He was buried in a tomb. In submitting to all this, everything needed to satisfy the judgment and justice of God was satisfied in Jesus.

I love the line from an old song that says, "broader than the scope of my transgression." Anything that any human can do is addressed in the work of the Cross. There is nothing you can do that disqualifies you from the free gift of forgiveness and salvation.

Those Who Love Much

The account of the woman who anointed Jesus' feet demonstrates how the love and forgiveness of Jesus will profoundly affect a person.

> I tell you, her sins—and they are many—have been forgiven, so she has shown me much love. But a person who is forgiven little shows only little love.
>
> —Luke 7:47 NLT

This dear woman must have had a significantly dysfunctional lifestyle. She would have not only committed great sin but also had terrible things imposed on her, and she would have felt the weight of sin—both her own sin as well as the effects of the sin of others.

She therefore had a great deal to thank Jesus for. The weight of her sin would have been almost in equal proportion to the love and thankfulness she had toward Jesus.

Jenny's Story

My friend Jenny, whom I've prayed with for many years, was blessed to grow up in a Christian home, and she loved Jesus all her life. She said that she can't remember a time when she didn't love Jesus. She had been a good child and didn't really have a testimony of coming to Jesus out of a lifestyle of sin and debauchery. That was a challenge to her. She told me, "I found it difficult to accept the idea that my thankfulness to

Jesus could only be as great as the amount of sin that had shown up in my life." After all, how much sin could be at work in the life of a young child?

This woman in Luke 7:47 was forgiven a great deal. She loved Jesus immensely because she was forgiven much. But Jenny also loved Jesus so much. Was her love somehow limited because she had not been so terribly bad?

When Jenny was about 11 years old, she actually did do something terrible. There was a boy in her class who had a lettering card for tracing letters. Jenny recalls, "It was an amazing piece of stationery, and I wanted it so badly. So I took it. I slipped it into my school bag, brought it home, and hid it under my bed."

But she couldn't sleep that night. That little lettering card felt like it was burning a hole through her mattress. It seemed to be calling out to her from under the bed. She knew she had done wrong, and she knew God was not pleased.

The next morning, Jenny jumped on her bike and rode straight to her classmate's house. She slipped the card into his letterbox as quickly as she could. What a relief! The fear she had felt wasn't fear of her classmate finding out or even of her mother discovering what she'd done. It was fear of God. She confessed, "The sense of separation from Him was more than my little 11-year-old heart could bear."

Returning the card wasn't enough; Jenny needed to repent before God. And when she did, peace flooded back in. It was not the act of stealing itself that was significant. It was the separation from God that put her in the same category as the woman in Luke 7:47. Jenny had been forgiven an enormous amount, and she was so very thankful. She had felt the weight of her sin as separation from God, even as a child, and she never wanted to feel that again.

Sin Is Not a "Spectrum Disorder"

Sin is sin. It's not a range of degrees from not too bad to unforgivable. Sin is not a spectrum disorder. The definition of a "spectrum disorder" is that it may represent a range of symptoms in severity, comprising "severe" disorders through to "mild and nonclinical deficits."

The severity of sin is not on a sliding scale. Some people may think, "A little bit is okay. A whole lot is more severe." Some may think that a large amount of sin deserves more judgment, but little bits can be excused. But God's judgments are true, sin is sin—little or lots. God doesn't say, "Well, it's okay. No one was really hurt. I'll let it go this time." No, *all* have sinned and fall short of the glory of God.

> ...For there is no difference; for all have sinned and fall short of the glory of God.
>
> —Romans 3:22-23 NKJV

Sin—Without God

Sin is often seen as "an offense against religious or moral law" or "a transgression of the law of God." But a more accurate definition would be "a vitiated (faulty or defective) state of human nature in which the self is estranged from God."

That's a good definition of sin—"a faulty or defective state of human nature in which the self is estranged from God." Literally, sin is being "without God." In fact, we get the English word *sin* from the Latin word *sine* meaning "without."

Being without God, or being estranged from God, has fruit—the fruit of sin. The real condition is the condition of the heart being without God. As a consequence, a multitude of sinful deeds will emanate from your life.

> In those days you were living apart from Christ. You were excluded from citizenship among the people of Israel, and you did not know the covenant promises God had made to them. You lived in this world without God and without hope. But now you have been united with Christ Jesus. Once you were far

> away from God, but now you have been brought near to him through the blood of Christ.
>
> —Ephesians 2:12-13 NLT

Being without God is being without hope. In that condition, you will be subjected to His judgment, whether the deed is little or great.

The blood of Jesus cures your condition of being estranged from God. It brings you back to God. You may make mistakes, but you no longer live "in sin." You're redeemed from the faulty condition of being without God.

> But now in Christ Jesus you who once were far off have been brought near by the blood of Christ.
>
> —Ephesians 2:13 NKJV

You and I can therefore give great praise, and our praise is as deep and as wide as the mercy we have received. We were forgiven for the brokenness of our human condition, forgiven for the emptiness of being without God. You and I can be so thankful for that!

Only God Has the Right to Judge

The first sin in the Garden of Eden occurred when Adam and Eve ate from the tree of the knowledge of good and evil. Before this act, they lived in a state of innocence, walking with God and trusting His guidance completely. Everything they knew came from God; all they saw was good, and they relied entirely on His wisdom and authority. But then Satan came on the scene. He challenged God's authority and threw out this to Eve:

> "You won't die!" the serpent replied to the woman. "God knows that your eyes will be opened as soon as you eat it, and you will be like God, knowing both good and evil."
>
> —Genesis 3:4-5 NLT

Well, you most probably know the story. They ate the fruit, their eyes were opened, and they gained the knowledge to distinguish between good and evil. They could now make judgments for themselves, assessing right and wrong, good and evil, something that had previously been God's purview alone. The serpent's temptation was no idle trick—it was true. By eating the fruit, Adam and Eve stepped into a new reality. They became like God, who is Judge. They could now judge, but they judged as rebels. Judgment is God's domain alone.

From that moment on, humanity carried the knowledge of good and evil, which profoundly affected our relationship with God and with one another. This knowledge of good and evil causes us to make judgments and assessments that do not align with God's perspective.

God Judges Through Jesus

God alone ultimately makes righteous judgment. Praise God for the work of redemption. God now judges us through the finished work of Jesus. As a result, we are called not to judge others based on what we see with our eyes but to know them as God sees them. Likewise, we are not to judge nations, rulers, or anyone in authority, or to make any assessment at all, without first seeking God's insight and perspective.

> And to Jesus, the Mediator (Go-between, Agent) of a new covenant, and to the sprinkled blood which speaks [of mercy], a better and nobler and more gracious message than the blood of Abel [which cried out for vengeance].
>
> —Hebrews 12:24 AMPC

The blood of Abel calls for vengeance, but the blood of Jesus calls for mercy. There is a righteous judgment that answers the call for justice and vengeance arising from the cry of spilled human blood. But the blood of Jesus has a cry of a better covenant. His sprinkled blood speaks of mercy. That's a better and nobler and more gracious message!

The question therefore is, "Whose blood are you representing?" Are you calling for vengeance or calling with the voice of Jesus for mercy? The new covenant calls for us to see what God sees and to call for mercy, not vengeance. God's judgment will come, but for this season let's call out for mercy.

Are you calling for vengeance or calling with the voice of Jesus for mercy?

In this age of grace, the judgment of God has been satisfied in Jesus so God can righteously extend mercy. Even angels do not pronounce judgment—not even on demons.

> Yet Michael the archangel, when contending with the devil he disputed about the body of Moses, dared not bring against him a reviling accusation, but said, "The Lord rebuke you!"
>
> —Jude 1:9 NKJV

But You, Beloved

A definition of mercy is compassion or forgiveness shown toward someone whom it is within one's power to punish or harm.

When we call for mercy, it's not our own mercy that we extend. The power to give mercy is with the one who has the power to harm, or in this case, to judge. We have no power or authority to judge, that's God's place. But we have been given the authority to cry out to God for His mercy to be extended to people who need mercy. Authority that has been delegated to me allows me to extend God's mercy.

There are two powerful verses in the book of Jude that we use often when teaching about prayer, especially praying in the spirit. If you are a pray-er, you know those verses:

> But you, beloved, building yourselves up on your most holy faith, praying in the Holy Spirit, keep yourselves in the love of God, looking for the mercy of our Lord Jesus Christ unto eternal life.
>
> —Jude 1:20-21 NKJV

But let's look at that verse in context:

> Now Enoch, the seventh from Adam, prophesied about these men also, saying, "Behold, the Lord comes with ten thousands of His saints, to execute judgment on all, to convict all who are ungodly among them of all their ungodly deeds which they have committed in an ungodly way, and of all the harsh things which ungodly sinners have spoken against Him."
>
> These are grumblers, complainers, walking according to their own lusts; and they mouth great swelling words, flattering people to gain advantage. But you, beloved, remember the words which were spoken before by the apostles of our Lord Jesus Christ: how they told you that there would be mockers in the last time who would walk according to their own ungodly lusts. These are sensual persons, who cause divisions, not having the Spirit.
>
> But you, beloved, building yourselves up on your most holy faith, praying in the Holy Spirit, keep yourselves in the love of God, looking for the mercy of our Lord Jesus Christ unto eternal life.
>
> —Jude 1:14-21 NKJV

Here and even further back in this chapter, Jude talks about all the people who deserve judgment. The list is quite lengthy! Egypt, Sodom and Gomorrah and those who practice sexual perversion, fallen angels, those who claim authority from dreams, scoffers, Cain, Balam, Korah, grumblers, complainers, braggers. It's quite a list! God will judge these people. In verse 14, he says that God will come at the right time to execute judgment on all these people.

We could stop right there and say, "Oh, that's a good thing! We are so with You, God! All these sinners need judgment, and it couldn't come soon enough!"

But that's not what Jude exhorts us to do. In verse 20 (NLT), he uses a big BUT! "*But* you, dear friends, must build each other up in your most holy faith." Why? Because what God has for you to do in these difficult times requires great faith and the leading of the Holy Spirit.

Then he says, while you are praying in the Holy Spirit, usually associated with tongues, look for something. Look in your heart for an element of God. It's an element of His character and person, which is love. And while you are there, in His love, look for mercy. Mercy is there in your heart too. God is there; and if God is there, so is His love and His mercy.

Then Jude goes on to say:

> And you must show mercy to those whose faith is wavering. Rescue others by snatching them from the flames of judgment. Show mercy to still others, but do so with great caution, hating the sins that contaminate their lives.
>
> —Jude 1:22-23 NLT

Show mercy. Whose mercy? God's mercy.

Mercy Triumphs over Judgment

> For to him who has shown no mercy the judgment [will be] merciless, but mercy [full of glad confidence] exults victoriously over judgment.
>
> —James 2:13 AMPC

> For judgment is without mercy to the one who has shown no mercy. Mercy triumphs over judgment.
>
> —James 2:13 NKJV

We use our words to call for mercy. When we see things that deserve judgment, look for the mercy of God. It's there because God is there in you.

How many times have we seen kids in the streets on skateboards without helmets, acting like hooligans. What's your response? Is it to call them out as hooligans, or is it to call for the mercy of God? "Dear

When we see things that deserve judgment, look for the mercy of God.

God, have mercy on that young man. Save him and take him to his destiny and purpose in You. Angels, you go with him and protect him."

When you see police officers on duty, call for mercy. "God, protect them and harden them against corruption. Send angels to help them do their God-given job."

When you see politicians speaking in public, and what they are saying grates on you, call for mercy. "God help them and grant them wisdom that comes from You. Have mercy on them!"

Don't pronounce a curse when you see something deserving of judgment. Extend mercy. Don't retain a person's sin by holding it to them with your words. Don't just use your authority to shout at the devil. Take your authority, using words of life to extend mercy.

> And when He had said this, He breathed on them, and said to them, "Receive the Holy Spirit. If you forgive the sins of any, they are forgiven them; if you retain the sins of any, they are retained."
>
> —John 20:22-23 NKJV

Love Mercy

In these days, the whole world is groaning under the weight of sin. There will come a time when the door for mercy will start to close and the judgments of God cannot be held back any longer. God is looking for people who will be the Church, who will represent Him perfectly. God is looking for a people who will extend His mercy to those who are in need of it.

Can you imagine what your city would look like if mercy were extended?

Can you imagine if your government were covered in the mercy of God?

> He has shown you, O man, what is good; and what does the Lord require of you but to do justly, to love mercy, and to walk humbly with your God?
>
> —Micah 6:8 NKJV

When it's up to you, do justly. For every other instance, love mercy—extend and dispense it. Mercy triumphs over judgment.

11

THE SPIRIT OF PROPHECY

The prophetic of God has continuity. It isn't just a spurt of prophecy here and a spurt of prophecy there. It's all a story. It's all a plan. It's all strategic. What He is giving is connected to what He has given. It isn't going to contradict. It isn't going to just be completely random. There's going to be continuity, and the more that we see that about the ways and the purposes of God, we see just how complex they are. They're grand and glorious and unfathomable.

—Patsy Cameneti, 2025

The "spirit of prophecy" is very intriguing. It has about it an element of the spectacular, the mystical, the operation of the ways of God in the spirit realm. The "spirit of prophecy" is a phrase referring to divine insight and guidance, particularly the ability to receive and share prophetic messages from God. It could be called "inspired utterance" or the utterance of God. He breathes into the human spirit, and we breathe it out through our mouth in the form of words. It is inspired by God.

He breathes into the human spirit, and we breathe it out through our mouth in the form of words.

New Testament Prophecy

In the New Testament age, prophecy is defined more as "forthtelling" rather than "foretelling." *Forthtelling* is to speak out by divine utterance the word of the Lord that is for that moment or situation. *Foretelling* was seen more in the Old Testament, when the word of the Lord often came with a warning and a prediction of what was to come. But the underlying theme of all prophecy is to speak under divine inspiration and utterance.

Jesus' Testimony

A key biblical definition of prophecy is from Revelation 19:10 that states, "the testimony of Jesus is the spirit of prophecy." This means that all genuine prophecy is centered on Jesus Christ and is ultimately a revelation of His person and work. It has in its essence the "Alpha and Omega" of Jesus. He is at the beginning and at the end.

> ...Worship God! For the substance (essence) of the truth revealed by Jesus is the spirit of all prophecy [the vital breath, the inspiration of all inspired preaching and interpretation of the divine will and purpose, including both mine and yours].
>
> —Revelation 19:10 AMPC

Old Testament Prophets

Even the prophets of old, when they spoke by divine utterance, gave witness to the continuum of a prophetic line of words that ultimately pointed to Jesus—His first coming and His return.

The Old Testament prophets were somehow, by faith, able to dip into the dispensations that were to come; and as they did, they saw shadows and forms of what would be in those upcoming dispensations.

The roles and functions of Old Testament prophets were activated by divine commission. This included public proclamation of the will and plans of God, which often included warnings. But even the warnings came with a message of hope that if the people repented and turned from their sinful ways, God would forgive and restore.

Prophets were used by God to deliver His message, which involved publicly denouncing sin and oppression while also foretelling future judgment. All prophecy was pointed toward getting a people ready for the coming of the Messiah.

The Spirit Upon

In the Old Testament, the anointing, or the prophetic word, would come *upon* the prophet or the person. The Bible says that they spoke or wrote as God moved on them. The word to note here is *upon*, or *on*; it was not *within*. There are also examples of kings, such as King Saul, who lay on the ground and prophesied all day. He was not a prophet. He was not even a good king at that time. Yet the anointing came on him to prophesy.

Desire to Prophesy

In the New Testament, or this age of grace, we have the Holy Spirit as an inward resident. It is possible for us, as new covenant believers, to receive prophetic utterance from God at any time, because the Spirit of the living God is now *in* us, not just on us. Now that has some amazing potential!

Paul wrote to the church at Corinth and said that every one of them may prophesy. He actually encouraged them to seek to prophesy. That doesn't mean that next Sunday you need to rush into a pulpit. There are times, such as in prayer or even across the table from a friend, that a spirit of prophecy can come on you.

The testimony of Jesus is the spirit of prophecy. At times when I have been talking to someone on an airplane about Jesus, just testifying about what Jesus has done in my life, a spirit of prophecy comes on me, and I am inspired to witness. It is very simple in its nature, but nonetheless it is the spirit of prophecy.

Ordinary believers can prophesy. Even in the Old Testament, in 2 Chronicles 20, one stood up in the midst of the congregation. It was not the one at the front; he was from the midst of the congregation. He gave an amazing battle plan that preachers use as whole sermon texts today, and it originated in the midst of the congregation. The spirit of prophecy came upon him.

If Paul encourages us all to desire to prophesy, it must be available to all of us because we have the Spirit of God in us.

We know that singers and musicians also can operate in the spirit of prophecy. When they are yielded to God and not just going by what they have prepared, something can come out of their mouth, or from their instrument, that they did not plan or practice. That is the spirit of prophecy.

This can happen for you as well. It is possible for the Spirit of God to move on anyone who is yielded to the Spirit. Anyone!

Does God Have Exclusive Use?

Did you know that God doesn't have exclusive use of believers? How can that be? Have you ever been tempted to say some things that are not edifying, not compassionate, not in accordance with the Word of God? Actually, have you been tempted to say something that may have even been inspired by the devil? Now hold that in your mind and think about this.

> When Jesus came into the region of Caesarea Philippi, He asked His disciples, saying, "Who do men say that I, the Son of Man, am?" So they said, "Some say John the Baptist, some Elijah, and others Jeremiah or one of the prophets." He said to them, "But who do you say that I am?" Simon Peter answered and said, "You are the Christ, the Son of the living God." Jesus answered

> and said to him, "Blessed are you, Simon Bar-Jonah, for flesh and blood has not revealed this to you, but My Father who is in heaven."
>
> —Matthew 16:13-17 NKJV

Peter received a direct revelation. He spoke by inspiration. Jesus said, "Flesh and blood has not revealed this to you but My Father in heaven." God Himself revealed that to Peter.

Yet just six verses later, it was a very different matter. Jesus was talking about how He needed to go up to Jerusalem and that He would be taken and suffer terrible things. Peter responded by saying, "No, Lord, this cannot be so." What did Jesus say to Peter, the same man who just a few verses earlier Jesus had called blessed? Did Jesus say, "Get thee behind Me, Peter?" Or did He say, "Get thee behind Me lying spirit?" No, the one who spoke through Peter was not a little demon, it was Satan himself! In one verse, God Almighty was speaking through Peter, and six verses later, Satan himself is inspiring Peter to speak!

> Jesus turned to Peter and said, "Get away from me, Satan! You are a dangerous trap to me. You are seeing things merely from a human point of view, not from God's." Then Jesus said to his disciples, "If any of you wants to be my follower, you must give up your own way, take up your cross, and follow me."
>
> —Matthew 16:23-24 NLT

How can it be that the inspiration for Peter was Satan himself? Peter was simply expressing his heartfelt desire. How bad could that be? Satan was using something very natural and even logical that was coming from Peter's mind. It wasn't some weird doctrine or an obvious lie. Peter spoke from his own natural understanding and limited

We must give up our own perspective and ways of thinking and operate just as Jesus did.

perspective. He was seeing from a human point of view. That's what Satan used to try and influence Jesus' journey to the Cross.

We can take stern warning from that example! If we are to be true followers of Jesus, used to speak the oracles of God, we must give up our own perspective and ways of thinking and operate just as Jesus did. He did nothing from Himself but only what He heard and saw from His Father. I never want to be inspired of the devil to work against God's plans!

Who Uses Your Voice?

A person's voice is like a microphone. It is not for exclusive use of anyone. There have been born-again people in churches who have been double agents. The devil wanted to say something, and they have just opened their mouth and blabbed it out for him. When the devil has wanted to cause division in the Church, he didn't have to send in someone from the outside. He just moved on someone to open their mouth and utter all sorts of devilishly inspired utterance. They have been double agents in the kingdom of God!

When my girls were little, they were learning to play the piano. I was teaching them the duets that I learned as a little girl. Our piano would sound out anything we would play, mistakes and all. But that same piano could also have surrendered to the fingers of a master pianist. It would have been the same piano, but it would have made a completely different sound!

Has the devil ever used somebody in our kingdom to work against our kingdom? Pray to God that he's never used you in that way!

What about Ananias and Sapphira in Acts? It says, "Why have you let Satan fill your heart? You lied to the Holy Spirit…" (Acts 5:3 NLT). They died for it. They were Christians in the Church, and Satan convinced those two people to collaborate in a lie. And God said they had lied to Him.

What about the disciples when some people were not accepting Jesus. They said, "Master, let's call fire down from heaven." Jesus "rebuked them." He said in essence, "You don't know by what spirit you speak" (Luke 9:55). These were close disciples of Jesus. Did the devil use people who were walking close to Jesus? Obviously, yes!

God Uses Kings and All in Authority

We have seen that those in civil seats of authority are called "ministers" in Romans 13. They are God's ministers, and God can use them to speak His words. However, just as with Christians, God does not have exclusive use of good kings or rulers; the devil does not have exclusive use of mean and hard-hearted kings or rulers. Neither kingdom has exclusive use of any person in a position of authority.

You may ask, "Well, who gets to use these rulers?" The answer is simple. Whoever claims the use of them. If the Church does not claim them, by default, many things have just gone over to the god of this world.

The Church, however, is now being raised up by God to prepare the way of the Lord, and we are claiming the use of these positions of authority and influence.

Let's look a little at another example. What about Caiaphas? Caiaphas was the one who helped incite the people to yell "Crucify Him!" at Jesus' trial. He was the high priest of the time. In the middle of Jesus' trial and crucifixion, Caiaphas prophesied. He said, "It's better for you that one man should die for the people than for the whole nation to be destroyed" (John 11:50 NLT). Then the scripture says that "he did not say this on his own" (John 11:51 NLT) but by the Spirit of God as the High Priest. He was not inspired of God to do most of the things he did, but he had this moment of inspiration, and he spoke by prophecy. The next moment he was just as ugly and wicked as the moment before he prophesied.

What about King Saul in 1 Samuel 19? He was trying to kill David! Saul was eaten up with jealousy, so he sent some people to go get David. They arrived to where the sons of the prophets were. These people who had murder in their eyes, ready to kill David, started to prophesy!

That frustrated Saul, so he sent some more people to kill David. These people also started to prophesy when they got around the sons of the prophets.

So Saul said he would go himself. He arrived there with the prophets, and he too started prophesying. He lay on the ground all day long and prophesied! Then he got up and started hunting David again.

We think that people have to be perfect before they can prophesy. And generally speaking, it is good to consecrate yourself and be a prepared vessel whom God can speak through. But we see that God can speak through anyone or anything. What amazing potential there is for the plan of God! God, being God, is able to use any vessel. That puts the devil at a great disadvantage!

There are people who would be astounded if they knew they were being a megaphone for the devil. That's not what they would want; nevertheless, they are working as double agents, bringing pain, division, and disrepute. Something comes on them, and they yield to it! Many times, it's just like Peter. They simply are seeing things merely from a human point of view, not from God's.

So if Satan can use people in our kingdom to work against our kingdom, even well-meaning people, why can't God use somebody in the kingdom of darkness against the kingdom of darkness for His purposes? He can, and He does! Something can come on them too—the hand of God—and they yield to it!

I was at a prayer conference in Bonn, Germany, and the Lord made some things clear to me when I was there. I saw in my spirit that if the body of Christ will pray, the spirit of prophecy will come upon people even though they are set for the destruction of the kingdom of God. There will be a moment when they will speak by the Spirit of God. Just like Caiaphas did against Jesus, they will speak for our kingdom.

The voice of God could get into government offices this way, and people who had bad counsel will forget what they were going to say and by the Holy Spirit come out with something different and in line with the will and plans of God.

I saw it happening! It can happen across the board! I believe it will happen in all the places we pray. But I tell you, the setting where I saw it happening was the European Union!

When I saw this, I just squealed with delight, and I took note. God said to me that the European Union would be a vehicle in the time to come for the antichrist. He is not in that position of authority just yet, but the pieces to the mechanism are coming together.

Before I saw that, I remember watching the European Union coming together and thinking, *Oh God! This is terrible!* But after that day, I saw great possibilities!

Why would we withhold our prayers from positions of authority and by default turn them over to the devil? Let's dispense wisdom, light, and power to those in positions of great influence.

Sometimes when we have seen that something is bad, we have held back our prayer, but actually 1 Timothy 2:1-2 tells us to pray *for* the government. Instead of leaning away, lean into that place in prayer.

In one of our prayer groups at church, we were praying for our current Australian Prime Minister. Many people in this nation disagree with his politics and social agenda. He has been the brunt of jokes and memes and it's so easy to get caught up in the foolish jesting.

In that prayer meeting, the Lord dealt with us about that. He said we would never be in a position to pray for him if we got involved in foolish jesting. If we really want God to use the mouth of our Prime Minister to speak the utterance of God, how could we pray for him when we actually dishonor him? In doing that, we are resisting what God has established. So we repented, dispensed honor on him, and prayed for him to be inspired by God in his seat of authority.

Together and individually, we have prayed for many political leaders and people of influence whom we don't like. We have a biblical responsibility to do that. Perhaps we would like to see them ousted and have someone in power who may be more in line with our Christian ethos, but if we believe what is written in Romans 13:2, we will not resist them. We pray *for* these leaders and bestow honor on them. They need it!

Lean Into the Bad Places

Aren't you glad that Jesus didn't lean *away* from the world when He saw that we were all going to hell? Aren't you glad that God sent Him *into* the world? He came right here to a lost and dying world. Jesus came into the bad place!

Governmentally speaking, we have to lean into the bad places. Members of the body of Christ around the world are also strengthened by our prayers. When we pray, those who have lowered their rod of authority, or don't even know they have one, can then be strengthened to lift up their authority.

There are some countries in the world where the believers don't know even a fragment of what you know. We can really help them lift up their hands and pray for their nation victoriously. Be like Aaron and Hur who strengthen the arms that hang down. Call to them in prayer to strengthen those feeble knees. Pray for them to stand up and not get weary under their government, to rise up and take their place beside the right hand of the throne of God.

Let's make Jesus happy so that what He did was not just nice for a few people in the Church. The Church is not to be weak in any place of the world. Let's help them!

We are to take His victory and enforce it in the whole earth. Enforce it in your life, yes, but enforce it any way the Holy Spirit points you. Lean into those dark places and expect that the Spirit of God will come into those places.

When we pray for all those in civil authority, they will end up working into the plan of God. Our prayer can make "Something" come upon them. The words God uses them to say will add to the plan of God for the coming of the Lord. The Spirit of Prophecy can move on people in those places, and the plan of God will be unfolded on earth as it is in heaven.

PART FOUR

KINGDOM CONTEXT

As citizens of the kingdom of God, we have a mission to bring to earth what already exists in heaven. Part of that mission is to pray for kings and all in authority so that all people will be saved and come to the knowledge of the truth. But we do it as kingdom citizens, not just as citizens of our natural nation.

12

THE ROLE OF THE CHURCH

[The purpose is] that through the church the complicated, many-sided wisdom of God in all its infinite variety and innumerable aspects might now be made known to the angelic rulers and authorities (principalities and powers) in the heavenly sphere.

—Ephesians 3:10 AMPC

Raised to Sit with Him

Because of the intention of God to have His plan worked in the earth, He made us His body on the earth when He raised Jesus from the dead. Jesus is the Head, but there's no function of God in the earth without His body. The devil knows this, so he does everything he can to stop that function. Even though we have legal, theological, true reality seating with Jesus in heavenly places, we don't have function there unless we're aware of it.

So the devil and those lying principalities will do everything they can to create doubt concerning our awareness of our seating. They use tricks and lies to try to confuse and deceive us.

The devil needs you to *not* function from your seat, so he'll get you into strife; he'll get you sad; he'll pull you under. The devices of the kingdom of darkness are so devious that they may even make you think it is all just normal. Because you are here on earth and you are human, they make you claim that earthly identity as your primary identity. And if you claim that as your primary identity, you're neutered. Powerless! You won't act like a child of the living God at all. You may sing about power and sing about might, but there just won't be any. That kind of life really dishonors the work of Jesus.

Light of the World

If we are going to work together with God, not only as citizens of this country but also as citizens of heaven, then we must acknowledge the seating He paid so much for us to have. Our seating as a heavenly citizen is our primary position and identity.

Our seating as a heavenly citizen is our primary position and identity.

From that seat we work together with the Holy Spirit to bring truth into the earth. That's the only seat that can have true and lasting effect. Truth sheds light in every area, not only in our own personal lives but also into civil, social, legal, financial and all arenas in our nation. We work together here on earth as the body, being the function and expression of the Head.

Dispensers of Light

We are also a light set on a hill. We are dispensers of light in a dark place. Jesus said this about Himself: "I am the light of the world" (John 8:12; 9:5 NKJV). But then He said, "You are the light of the world" (Matthew 5:14 NKJV).

A single light can be amazing in a dark place. But when you put His light and our lights together, it makes a brighter, more brilliant light, affecting a greater radius of people. When a church family's lights come together, the effect is a dispensation of light that has a heavenly quality and can go into even the darkest nooks and crannies.

The reason we congregate is not just for ourselves. Yes, we do experience the love of God in greater measure when we are together (Ephesians 3:18). But as the light of the world, we are meant to get out to the people. God has great intention for the people of earth—His love and redemption, and that cannot be legislated by government or civil authorities. It cannot be forced upon people. It must be emulated and dispensed through the Church, through the members of the body of Christ, as light in a dark place. He is in us not just to help us personally. He is in us to accomplish His will *through* us for the people of every nation.

It should make a difference that we, as the Church, are still here on the earth.

Dispensers of Truth

Truth makes people free. There are ways to dispense truth, not forcing it on people, but dispensing it so that people have access to the light, to the truth. Remember, the more people who choose to submit to God, the less influence those corrupt spirit beings have in our region and our nation.

Paul said in 1 Timothy 2:1-4 that God wants everybody to be saved. He essentially said, "That's why I was sent as an apostle and a teacher of the Gentiles, to proclaim the message of faith."

Well, you say, "I'm not an apostle." No, maybe you're not. But we *are* those who share the same great commission from the Lord Jesus Christ: go into all the world, preach the gospel and make disciples. It is an apostolic sending and purpose for our lives, even if it isn't an apostolic gifting. We live under a commission that sends us to preach the gospel of this kingdom to every creature so that His truth can make people free.

And in that sending, there are ways we can actively and efficiently dispense His truth, His love, and His purpose.

Extinguish the Darkness

I was thinking about fire blankets. I looked at some YouTube clips on how they are used. They are devices used to smother, or cover, a fire. I've never had to use one, but those blankets are really excellent safety items to have. Most of us have seen fire extinguishers but maybe don't know how a fire blanket works. I didn't, so I watched how to use one of these blankets on YouTube.

It showed a kitchen fire in a pan. Once the fire ignites, it starts building and growing in seconds. The man went over to the blanket that was in a packet hanging on the kitchen wall. I thought, *It's red and ugly; I don't know if anyone would actually hang one of those for nice decor.* Then the man took it out and showed how to use it.

All the while the fire was building in the pan on the stove; the man was so calm. He wasn't hollering, "Fire! Fire! Everybody run!" He very calmly approached the stove, laid the blanket over the pan, and then stepped back. The blanket did the work. It overcame what was in the pan and extinguished the flames.

I thought about this relating to we who cooperate with God for all people to be saved—those of your nation, with differing opinions, with different passions and all kinds of beliefs. Just like that blanket smothered and extinguished the fire, our prayers can smother and extinguish the fires that the kingdom of darkness wants to see take hold to destroy.

Sometimes we want to just clump and congregate together in church or in our home groups. That's nice, and it's so comfortable, but what He really wants us to do is *infiltrate* the world and make a difference. And that's how we can approach it—calmly, effectively, and with faith—like that blanket, letting God's power do the work through us.

Paul said, "Do not be overcome with evil" (Romans 12:21 NKJV). How do we approach evil? Do we make war on evil with every opportunity? Pray against it? Speak out against it? Is that what the Bible says in Romans? No, it doesn't say that.

Paul said, "Do not be overcome with evil," and then he says, "but overcome evil with good."

The Greater One in us has the ability to overcome evil. What we have is greater than any evil. Even if there is wickedness, violence, unrest, or strife, what He is inside us is greater. And that is what can overcome—just like a fire blanket.

The key is dispensing it. We get it out of the package and put it on the fire so that what He is, and who He is, can make the difference.

Dispensers of Love

Just being here on earth as His body is going to provoke some things that are not fun. What happens when hate manifests? Hate will provoke you in the flesh, and it will try to pull you in. Hate makes you want to hate. If somebody hits you, it makes you want to retaliate. It's like trying to fight fire with fire. And that won't work, not if you want to put the fire out. But maybe you have the kind of personality that wants to retreat and hide, like a turtle, and do nothing. That won't deal with the hate either.

Romans 12:21-22 says *don't be overcome with evil.* Don't participate in it or become part of it.

Instead, overcome evil with what? With good.

Love is greater than hate, but love isn't just "schmaltzy" or soft and sweet. It's not just condoning. It's not just tolerance. It's not, "It's okay, everything's okay." That's not love.

Think about how much God so loved the world—a world lost in sin, enemies of God. God didn't just say, "Okay, everybody do your own thing." He didn't just tolerate the world's sin. He did something about it.

He didn't attack the sin. With His love He became the Sacrifice for sin. And He did that while we were still sinners (Romans 5:8). Amazing, isn't it?

Love is stronger. It does not fail; but love must be actively used to overcome hate. Like a fire blanket, love covers without excusing or condemning. Love extinguishes hate.

The God of Peace

As children of God, we have His love working in us. We know that for sure! But let's look at something else. Because Jesus is the Prince of Peace, we also have His peace at work in us.

Peace, just like love, is greater than strife. Peace is greater than disunity. Peace is greater than things that are fractured. Jesus is peace. He is the Prince of Peace.

Peace doesn't always seem like the strongest characteristic of God. We may think of peace as the pillow or the soft, feathery part of God. Peace is sweet. Peace is comfortable. But scriptures show that peace is far more powerful than that.

> Then you will experience God's peace, which exceeds anything we can understand. His peace will guard your hearts and minds as you live in Christ Jesus.
>
> —Philippians 4:7 NLT

> And let the peace that comes from Christ rule in your hearts. For as members of one body you are called to live in peace. And always be thankful.
>
> —Colossians 3:15 NLT

If peace is going to *rule* in your heart and mind, it can't just be something that has no strength. It's not something that just lays there, floating like a pillow. No! Peace is powerful, and it rules.

Romans 16:20 (NKJV) says, "The God of peace will crush Satan under your feet shortly…." The Bible describes God's character in many ways including love, power, and authority. But this verse notes that the God of peace will crush Satan, showing that God's peace is not passive or soft. It's strong! Strong enough to rule and strong enough to crush.

If peace is going to rule in your heart and mind, it can't just be something that has no strength.

Therefore, peace must be more powerful than what we've thought of before, and it is.

> These things I have spoken to you, that in Me you might have peace. In the world you shall have tribulation, but be of good cheer; I have overcome the world.
>
> —John 16:33 NKJV

In John 14:27 (NKJV) Jesus says, "Peace I leave with you, My peace I give to you; not as the world gives do I give to you...." He was getting ready to go away, telling His disciples that He was about to return to the Father. And He says that what He is going to give them is peace.

Peace doesn't seem like a very powerful protection to leave His disciples. Peace didn't really seem to be what they would need in the days to come. That promise could have been disconcerting, unless of course they knew that peace actually meant something powerful, like bulletproof armor or heavy artillery. If that was so, then what would peace actually do for them?

Look at Ephesians 6. After Paul goes through the armor of God—the helmet of salvation, the breastplate of righteousness, the belt of truth—he says our feet are shod with the gospel of peace.

Sometimes our concept of peace is like putting on soft, feathery house slippers. But soldiers don't wear slippers. The other day I saw a couple of soldiers on a plane. Neither were wearing soft, feathery slippers. They wore all their gear, including heavy boots. For a soldier, what's on their feet is crucial, especially if they are headed for battle.

Feet need to be strong. Feet need to endure heat, sharp objects, and rough terrain. That's what God is saying: "I'm going to give your feet the preparation of the gospel of peace." We have some powerful footwear! This spiritual footwear enables us to walk through anything without being harmed. So this peace is far more powerful than we often imagine. And the Prince of Peace lives on the inside of us.

Jesus and the Power of Peace

Take a look in Mark chapter 4. I'd like us to look at this story, starting in verse 35:

> On the same day, when evening had come, He said to them, "Let us cross over to the other side." Now when they had left the multitude, they took Him along in the boat as He was. And

> other little boats were also with Him. And a great windstorm arose, and the waves beat into the boat, so that it was already filling. But He was in the stern, asleep on a pillow….
>
> —Mark 4:35-38 NKJV

That's amazing! They woke Him and said, "Teacher, do You not care that we are perishing?"

You have to picture this: these guys are in a boat out on the sea, there's a storm, and the water that's supposed to be on the outside of the boat is now filling the boat inside with water. They finally had to wake Him up. It's amazing that Jesus was able to sleep through all of this!

They woke Him up and said, "Teacher, don't You care that we are perishing?"

> Then He arose and rebuked the wind, and said to the sea, "Peace, be still!" The wind ceased, and there was a great calm. But He said to them, "Why are you so fearful? How is it that you have no faith?" And they feared exceedingly, and said to one another, "Who can this be, that even the wind and the sea obey Him!"
>
> —Mark 4:39-41 NKJV

At times in scripture a body of water, or the waters, can refer to a mass of people.

When I look at this story in that context, I see that Jesus and His disciples are out among the people. Suddenly, a storm comes, and the "waters"—that is, the people—are riled up. What used to be calm is now dangerous. What Jesus did, I believe, is an example for us to know what to do right now—in our society, in our situation, and for our nation.

When Jesus woke up, He did two things:

First, He used His authority to rebuke the wind. The wind is something you cannot see. There are forces you can't see that blow in and influence masses of people. Some voices you can hear, some people you can see. But behind those, there are spiritual forces that stir up the waters, making people rage.

Jesus first addressed what could not be seen in the spirit realm. Jesus didn't rebuke the people; He rebuked the unseen influence. It may have been unseen to the disciples, but Jesus saw it, and when He saw it, He knew what to do with it. He had the authority to do it, too. That word *rebuked* is strong. Why? Because without the wind's influence, the sea would have been calm. He saw it, and He rebuked the wind. Remember, Jesus did nothing without first hearing from His Father. So He would have done exactly what His Father told Him to do.

If we see uprisings among people and see what is influencing them, by the authority and unction we have in Jesus' name, we can speak to that influence.

Second, Jesus didn't stop there. Exercising God's will for the people is not just about opposing what is wrong or coming *against* anything. Jesus also gave a positive, proactive solution. In Matthew 18:18 (NKJV), Jesus says, "Whatever you bind on earth will be bound in heaven, and whatever you loose on earth will be loosed in heaven."

After rebuking the wind, He spoke to the sea: *"Peace."* He applied that "fire blanket" of peace to the waters, and it calmed down. Praise the name of the Lord!

You and I have authority in Jesus' name to do the same. When you get the unction by the Holy Spirit, don't be reluctant to push back what is stirring up strife and apply peace that is greater than strife.

Dispense What You Have of God

So far we've only looked at love and peace, but there's more. You can dispense everything He is, too. You can speak the truth to a situation. Don't just talk about the problem. Dispense truth!

If you're in a depressing situation, you don't have to become part of that complaining, whining environment. You can carry the joy of the Lord right inside you. Don't keep Him in the package. Get Him out! Put joy on the fire.

Dispense whatever you have of Him, be it love, joy, peace, truth, or anything you know about Jesus, the Living Word. And do it by speaking, not just thinking or wishing. Use your voice and say it!

God strategically has you where He wants you throughout the week to dispense His power and presence.

13

FOR KINGS AND ALL IN AUTHORITY

When the righteous are in authority, the people rejoice; but when a wicked man rules, the people groan.

—Proverbs 29:2 NKJV

New Birth of Freedom

In the famous Gettysburg Address given in 1863, Abraham Lincoln said that this nation shall have a "new birth of freedom." When Abraham Lincoln gave that address, the nation had been not just cut, it was torn in two by the Civil War! There was a tremendous amount of division in the nation. He actually spoke into God's purpose for the nation of America to be united.

There can be political freedom; there can be a new wave of economic freedom, a burst of new energy in inventions and all kinds of different things. You can have access to all kinds of things in education, technology and finances, but people are still absolutely bound. You can be in a free country and still be bound. People are not truly free unless they are out of the kingdom of darkness. Freedom, true freedom, is found only in Jesus Christ.

I want to echo Abraham Lincoln's words. There is something that God wants for us to experience in this nation, in any nation where you may reside, and that is a new birth of freedom. Real freedom in Jesus!

People are not truly free unless they are out of the kingdom of darkness.

God's Strategy for True Freedom

Before Abraham Lincoln gave his monumental address, there were the founders and the writers of the American Constitution. Before that, however, someone spoke with even greater authority—words that will never, ever fade away. We hear from the Holy Spirit through the apostle Paul in 1 Timothy:

> I urge you, first of all, to pray for all people. Ask God to help them; intercede on their behalf, and give thanks for them. Pray this way for kings and all who are in authority so that we can live peaceful and quiet lives marked by godliness and dignity. This is good and pleases God our Savior, who wants everyone to be saved and to understand the truth. For, There is one God and one Mediator who can reconcile God and humanity—the man Christ Jesus. He gave his life to purchase freedom for everyone. This is the message God gave to the world at just the right time. And I have been chosen as a preacher and apostle to teach the Gentiles this message about faith and truth. I'm not exaggerating—just telling the truth.
>
> —1 Timothy 2:1-7 NLT

The Amplified Version lists different ways of praying: prayers, petitions, supplication, intercessions, and thanksgivings that would be made for all people. Then jump down to verse 4 and notice that God would have all people be saved and come to the knowledge of the truth.

Between verse 1 and verse 4 is God's strategy to help unfold His plan for all people. This strategy is to pray for kings and for all who are in authority so that we can lead quiet and peaceable lives in all godliness and dignity, honesty.

So, this is our strategy. Pray! If we're going to pray for all people, it must include praying for kings and for all who are in authority. These are the influencers of the people. But before he even gets to praying for kings and for all in authority, the first directive is to pray, be mindful, be aware of all people.

It is possible that you and I, or any other person, can become self-absorbed. You can get caught up in yourself, your family, your own world, your business, your school, your future, and everything that's happening in your life.

This passage of Scripture does something powerful. It does what God did for Abraham of old when He spoke to him one time in a field. He said, "Look up from the place where you now stand. Lift up your eyes and look."

First Timothy 2:4-6 does that for us. It lifts our eyes. It gets us out of our own kitchen and personal circle. It helps us to look beyond and see the people who are the target of God's love. The target of that love is *the whole world.* "God so loved the world."

All People to Be Saved

Paul told the church in Corinth that Jesus did what He did for *me*, but also for *the whole world.* Let's look at this scripture passage a little more closely:

> Who wants ***everyone to be saved*** and to understand the truth. For, there is one God and one Mediator who can reconcile God and humanity—the man Christ Jesus. ***He gave his life to purchase freedom for everyone***. This is the message God gave to the world at just the right time.
>
> —1 Timothy 2:4-6 NLT

Notice Jesus "gave his life to purchase freedom for everyone." Twice in just this short passage, we see that God's will, God's purpose, and God's intention are for *everyone* to be saved. Not only is it His will that everyone be saved, but the *price* necessary for everyone's salvation was already paid through the redemption Jesus accomplished in His death, burial, and resurrection.

"He wants everyone to be saved." That was the proof. God's desire is for all people to come to Him.

This is a God-given strategy. The more people are saved and brought into the kingdom of God, the less influence evil principalities have, and the kingdom of darkness is decreased.

Second, when we pray for kings and all in authority, God is able to influence those who sit in the seats of authority. These seats are ordained by God as we have seen in Romans 13. We see in that passage of scripture that those seats are set in place by God, and whoever sits in those seats will have influence over a whole population of people. And maybe not only a population but a whole demographic or grouping of people.

Wisdom from Above

That influence is given by God because of the seat they occupy. That seat needs wisdom from above. If wisdom from above is not dispensed, the occupants of the seat will default to wisdom from below.

Rulers need wisdom to rule, and they will seek for it and get it from one of two places.

> By me [wisdom] kings reign, and rulers decree justice. By me princes rule, and nobles, all the judges of the earth.
>
> —Proverbs 8:15-16 NKJV

James 3:15-17 says there are two kinds of wisdom—from below and from above. Rulers and those in authority certainly need the God-kind of wisdom. They depend on wisdom, and we must dispense God's wisdom for them by asking God to give it to them.

God is able to then influence whole populations of people through kings who rule and bring to bear God's influence. The key is the phrase in 1 Timothy 2:4-6 is *"everyone."* God wants all people to be saved and come to the knowledge of the truth.

Jesus died for all people and gave Himself as a ransom for all—everybody. This scripture is not just a suggestion. We are directed to pray for all people. But how do you pray for all, for all people? Do you just say, "God, just bless the whole world"? That is so cliché.

For Kings and All in Authority

If you want to pray for all people, you pray for kings and all in authority. When people are elected, they are raised to a place where their voice is elevated and influences more people. If you target them, they have influence over the people within their sphere.

That works for any kind of authority or place of influence. And it's not just people in politics; it's anyone who influences people. That would include musicians, movie stars, sports celebrities—anyone who influences other people. They have an elevated place where other people are looking at them. In that place they have an influence on those people.

You may say, "Well, what if those people are not good people?" Consider this. Who was in government at the time Paul wrote to Timothy? The Romans, and that empire wasn't exactly a Christian

For Kings and All in Authority

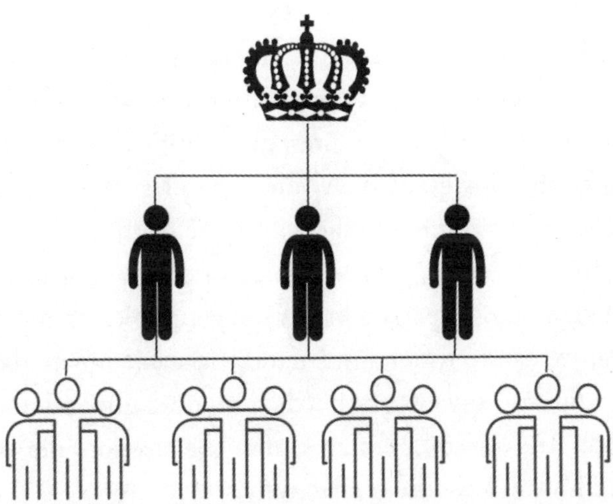

nation. I've lived in Rome! The city was built on seven hills dedicated to seven gods. It was never godly; it was a pagan place. And Nero wasn't exactly saved, sanctified, and filled with the Holy Ghost. No, Nero had some serious issues!

Paul's letter to Timothy was written from prison where in just a little while he was going to lose his head! But there is absolutely no indication in the epistles of Paul complaining or fault-finding about the government of his time.

Nero came and went. He might have been the strongest leader on the planet while he was there, but his influence lasted a short time. Paul knew there were more important things to talk about than political leaders. There are higher things to think about and to talk about.

We cannot change what was written in the Bible just because we live in another time. No, we're Christians, and the Bible is how we do things! So, what do we do for our leaders? We pray!

Citizen Responsibility

First Timothy 2 is not a political statement. It's a spiritual instruction to you as a citizen of heaven. It affects the nation you live in, but it is a work that is done from your position as a kingdom citizen.

Remember, you have dual citizenship. Being a citizen of your nation requires a different set of responsibilities and gives you certain rights. You have the right to vote and the responsibility to pay taxes. Even Jesus said to render to the governing authorities what is due (Matthew 22:21). Those kinds of rights and responsibilities are very precious, and we often take that for granted. A vote is a voice. And when everyone speaks, it gives great volume to the will of the people.

As a natural citizen, you have a voice, and you need to take advantage of this right and responsibility to use your voice on a natural level. We do what we can to foster a quiet and peaceable life marked by godliness and honesty. However, our civic duty does not end once we have cast our vote. The question remains: after the election, do we still have a voice, and how can we use it effectively?

We cannot simply elect someone to office and expect them to carry the full weight of responsibility. It's not enough to say, "Do your best. If things don't go well, I'll let you know at the next election."

From a national perspective, that might be where we stop. But as citizens of heaven, there's a deeper calling. God's agenda is not just about creating a good society. Our aim is not solely a wholesome or "Christian Nation."

We can vote against corruption, oppose wicked agendas, legislate for justice, care for the poor, and advocate for honest government. We can build a society where people live morally and do what is right. Yet, if these same people do not know Jesus Christ as their Lord and Savior, they still face an eternity separated from God.

Ultimately, God's goal is not just a wholesome, comfortable society. His purpose is that everyone comes to know the truth and is born again. This is God's heart. This is our commission.

A Quiet and Peaceful Life

Generally, when Christians pray and more people are brought into the kingdom, the nation will rise in righteousness. Godly leaders will be voted in, the freedom for the Church to operate will carry on unhindered, and the gospel of the kingdom will advance.

Here's an interesting twist, however. What about people who are Christians, love God, are filled with the Spirit, who pray for their nation and all in authority, but who live in nations where the government is corrupt? These precious people surely believe the Word of God and do what they are exhorted to do in 1 Timothy 2:1-7, yet they do not live in a nation that is "quiet and undisturbed." They live in a nation where they are persecuted, are in a minority group of believers or are even under the threat of martyrdom.

Is it because they are not praying hard enough, long enough, or do not have enough faith? Now that's a very valid question!

This became a question in the group of ladies I prayed with all these past years. The Lord then asked us the question. "Where do you find true peace?" Well, we knew that true peace is only found in Jesus. He is the Prince of Peace, and He promised He would leave His peace with us. We saw in a previous chapter that the peace He gives us is actually powerful and is able to "crush Satan under our feet."

So here's another way of looking at that portion of scripture:

> Pray this way for kings and all who are in authority so that we can live peaceful and quiet lives marked by godliness and dignity.
>
> —1 Timothy 2:2 NLT

"So that we can live peaceful and quiet lives" is the outcome of what? Is it the outcome of a good and righteous government—or is it the outcome of the fact that we pray? We know that the government is not the source of true, lasting, God-given peace. When we pray as we are directed in this verse, we can have confidence in God.

When we pray, we can enter His rest and our hearts and minds are at peace. Whatever is happening in our nation and government does not erode or compromise the peace we have because our trust is in God! *He* is the Source of our peace.

When we pray, we can enter His rest and our hearts and minds are at peace.

So, we pray, we intercede, we give thanks and make supplication to God on behalf of all people. We stay in peace and have our minds fixed on Him, listening for His words for the situation. In doing that, we utilize our heavenly citizenship and fulfill heaven's agenda.

Understand the Truth

God's will is that everyone be saved and come to the knowledge of the truth: "who wants everyone to be saved and to understand the truth" (1 Timothy 2:4 NLT). This fact is presented over and over. Let's look a little more at "truth."

The shepherd drives the wolf from the sheep, for which the sheep thank the shepherd as his liberator, while the wolf denounces him for the same act as the destroyer of liberty. Plainly, the sheep and the wolf have not agreed upon the definition of liberty.

The idea of truth is interesting. Some people may think that there are varying kinds of truth and that truth may be arbitrary. They think that their truth is their truth and your truth is your truth. Truth for some people may be different from truth for somebody else.

When Jesus stood before Pilate, He said that He came to bear witness to the truth. Pilate asked Jesus a very insightful question: "What is truth?" Pilate didn't realize he could actually reach out and touch the very personification of Truth Himself. Jesus *is* Truth personified.

People's interpretation of truth can be very interesting. The quotation from Abraham Lincoln in the box above is on my list of interesting quotes.

The definition of liberty could be the same as the definition of truth. There must be one absolute empirical definition.

Truth Frees People

Our quest for freedom, if it's outside of truth, will always put someone else in jeopardy. Somebody's freedom will come at someone else's expense unless that freedom has come by way of truth. Truth must be defined truly. It must be defined in who Jesus is and in what Jesus says.

A country that pursues freedom and liberty apart from truth will end up having some people free in their expression at the expense of others who become more bound. But a nation of people who come to freedom *through* truth are truly free!

Let me give you a really simple example I've experienced within the context of marriage. I talked to the Lord about my husband. I thought that if I told Him about my situation and the way I was handling things, He would take my side and I'd get my way. God would fix my husband for me.

I told the Lord all about the "truth" of the whole situation. But the Lord wouldn't even talk to me about my husband. He just started talking to me about me.

I would think, *Did You hear what I started this prayer with? Don't change the subject.* It was all inward. I wanted God to change my husband, but what the Lord did then was give me truth about me. It would make me free, but it would also bring freedom for our relationship.

Do you see how that works? It's never at the expense of somebody else. Truth lifts, and it lifts everyone. Praise the Lord!

There are many facts in the world, and the media will skew the facts to present facts as truth. These facts are subject to people's interpretations and also subject to change. The ultimate truth is found in Jesus. "Thy Word is truth."

Let's continue to pray for all people, especially for those in authority. This is part of God's strategy to have all saved and come to the knowledge of what is true—Jesus Himself.

14

KINGDOM CITIZENS

From one man he created all the nations throughout the whole earth. He decided beforehand when they should rise and fall, and he determined their boundaries. His purpose was for the nations to seek after God and perhaps feel their way toward him and find him—though he is not far from any one of us.

—Acts 17:26-27 NLT

Two Kingdoms

On this planet are many nations. Over time the borders shift and change, and the nations change, but there are always many nations. Spiritually speaking, however, there are only two kingdoms.

The kingdoms and nations of the world as we know them now will not always exist because they are not eternal kingdoms or nations. They come and go and eventually will come to an end. Jesus will judge the nations of the earth, and the kingdoms of this world will become the kingdoms of our God (Revelation 11:15-18).

There are two kingdoms, however, that are eternal kingdoms. They are not natural nations or kingdoms, and their landforms are not identifiable on a map. These are the kingdom of darkness and the kingdom of light.

The kingdom of darkness operates on lies and deception, but the kingdom of light operates on truth and light. The kingdom of darkness will end in eternal separation from God, but the kingdom of light is God's kingdom, and those who are in this kingdom will live on into eternity with Him.

The Great Rescue Operation

> For he has rescued us from the kingdom of darkness and transferred us into the Kingdom of his dear Son.
>
> —Colossians 1:13 NLT

I once met a businessman on a flight. I could tell he was a businessman by the way he was dressed. He had an accent, and I like to guess where people come from by their accent. He told me he was born in Eastern Europe and had lived under an oppressive government. When he was only 16, he decided to escape and he told absolutely no one, not even his family. He escaped into Italy, and it was a harrowing experience. Living on the streets, he was under the constant fear of capture. He ran from Italy to France by riding under a train. He joined the military and fought in World War II. One thing led to another, and he went to the United States of America, made a tremendous amount of money, and was finally able to bring his family to join him. It was quite a story!

These kinds of stories fascinate me. I love to read about people who escape from prison camps, from armies, and from nations. But at one time in history, from the kingdom of darkness, there was no possibility of escape—not ever! There was absolutely no way for any human to get out of this kingdom. The lord of this kingdom is awful and cruel, and members of this kingdom are under his domain. He is the lord of darkness—the devil. No one could ever get out of this kingdom by themselves. Someone had to come and get us out! We are so thankful that *Jesus* went into the kingdom of darkness and emerged to translate us into the kingdom of light!

A New Species of Human

While there are two eternal kingdoms on the earth, there are three groups of people. When someone is born again, the person is taken out of either the Jews or the nations and brought into the kingdom of God, the Church, the ecclesia, or the "called out ones."

Therefore, if you've been born again, you're actually a whole different species of human. I'm not trying to sound weird, but that's the truth! According to 2 Corinthians 5:17, you are a new species and a citizen of the kingdom of God. You will, however, still be a citizen of your natural birth by your natural descent. You will have the language and culture of the earthly citizenship you hold—your ethnos.

Every born-again believer will have this interesting tension, this curious dichotomy.

As born-again believers, we have a unique position of dual citizenship. We are now citizens of heaven, but how do we deal with the fact that we are also citizens of a natural nation? This interface causes tension because you have two citizenships, an earthly one and a heavenly one.

It takes the help of the Holy Spirit to recognize where you are and notice if you're functioning from your first birth reality (your ethnic or national identity) or if you're functioning from your second birth reality (the nature and identity of your citizenship in heaven). It will really help you if you can recognize the difference.

Kingdom Expansion

You can recognize a nation by its landform, but with the two eternal kingdoms, there is no landform. What then, makes up the landform of these kingdoms? Its people! People make up the form of each of these kingdoms. When you were in the kingdom of darkness, you were part of that form of that kingdom. You helped make up that kingdom. When you came out of that kingdom, you made that kingdom smaller! When you came into the kingdom of light, you made that kingdom bigger! You are now not just *in* light—you *are* light!

What we are about, our goal, is to diminish the kingdom of darkness and expand the kingdom of light, which is all done with people! The darkness gets smaller and light gets bigger. If you were the devil, would you just let that happen? No! You would fight that! And he does!

> For you are all children of the light and of the day; we don't belong to darkness and night.
>
> —1 Thessalonians 5:5 NLT

When you were first born as a baby, you were born into your nation. When you are born again, you are born into the kingdom of light; you become a citizen of this kingdom. You now hold dual citizenship. God uses your natural citizenship too, but your homeland is no longer this earth.

Our youngest daughter holds an American passport and is an American citizen, but she has never actually lived in America. We are citizens of the kingdom of heaven; we just haven't lived there yet.

We are citizens of the kingdom of heaven; we just haven't lived there yet.

The kingdom of God is in you. It's not a geographical location in the sky or somewhere out there. The kingdom of God cannot be confined just to heaven. Yes, heaven is your homeland but not yet your place of residence.

Sons and Daughters and Citizens

There are benefits and responsibilities of the natural kingdom or nation where you now live. There are also benefits and responsibilities of living in and being part of the kingdom of God.

When a child is born into a family, the first thing people look for is not the features of the nationality of the child. You look for the features of the parents. They may say, "Aww, he's got his daddy's nose," or, "So sweet, she's got her mama's eyes." The first reality that a child comes to know is not a national reality, it's a parent's love.

When people are born into the kingdom of God, their first identity doesn't revolve around kingdom identity. It revolves around a parental and family identity. So that's why when you are first born again, the very first thing you are called to be is a son or a daughter.

When someone is born again, we want to surround them first of all with the security of a family. They come to know God as their Father God. You never outgrow that identity. You grow up into it. Without that identity, you have a gap in your life. When a person is born again, the very first bond that needs to be established is with God. And the believer, just like the child, comes to know their own identity within that secure relationship.

As they grow, a young child begins to notice the world around them. They become aware of their family and friends, and beyond that is an awareness of their community, their city, and ultimately their nation.

Each child has unique rights based on what their family can offer them. They come to know that there are not only rights but also responsibilities that go with being a member of that family. Some children are very productive and responsible. But there are also children who are not so helpful. It doesn't mean they are not part of the family.

Even though children may not know they belong to a nation, they are still citizens. It's the same when we are born into the kingdom of God. We are not only born to be sons and daughters, but we are also born to be citizens, and with that come rights and responsibilities.

As we mature in this family, we become more aware of our rights and responsibilities as a citizen of the kingdom of God, just as a child becomes an adult and grows in awareness of their rights and responsibilities as a citizen of their own nation.

We are ambassadors for Christ here in this earth, in the nation we live in. We are also all missionaries, sent from the kingdom of heaven into this world.

National Tension

Abraham, who was called the Father of Faith, considered himself an alien or a foreigner because he was looking for a different land. Even when he walked through the land that God gave him, he considered himself a stranger to that land (Hebrews 11).

Some people, even though they are born again, never get to know their new kingdom identity. They cling strongly to the identity of their first birth only. They think their highest calling is a nationalistic fervor. That's where the tension lies.

There are some things about our natural or ethnic identity that we can and should celebrate—the culture, the food, the music, and so much more. But thank God for the truth! You have a higher identity, and even more importantly, you are no longer subject to the spiritual principalities and powers that seek to keep you bound in rituals and legal expectations of your "ethnos" that will end in death.

> Having disarmed principalities and powers, He made a public spectacle of them, triumphing over them in it. So let no one judge you in food or in drink, or regarding a festival or a new moon or sabbaths, which are a shadow of things to come, but the substance is of Christ.
>
> —Colossians 2:15-17 NKJV

In this passage, Paul was celebrating the truth that Jesus disarmed those principalities that once had you bound. Then he goes on to tell us to not allow people to judge us or hold over us any legal expectations related to culture or social expectations.

There are choices the Word of God gives you that are a snapshot of who you are, not according to your first birth but because of your second birth. It is vital to have a clear understanding of who you are now because you belong to God.

Advancing the Kingdom of God

When Jesus prayed the Lord's Prayer, He set out a wonderful pattern in prayer. He was praying that the kingdom of God would come, and it did come. He prayed that God's will, which already existed in heaven, would come to earth. It began unfolding as soon as Jesus prayed and is continuing even now.

We can still pray that prayer, and it will advance and increase the kingdom of God when we do. The kingdom of God is increased when more people come into it.

The kingdom of God is increased when more people come into it.

When we ask for the kingdom of God to be increased in a particular nation, what are we asking for? More churches to be built? No, not necessarily. We are literally asking for souls! Each day around the globe, people get saved!

When a person dies in any nation, they aren't taxed anymore by the government. The same is true spiritually. It's a blessed thing to die to our sins! We should celebrate our death to the kingdom of darkness every day. That kingdom no longer has any claim on born-again believers. We are dead to sin and alive in Christ Jesus!

Jesus' ministry was always attached to expanding the kingdom of God. And now you are part of that ministry.

15

PREPARING HIM A BODY

For because of Him the whole body (the church, in all its various parts), closely joined and firmly knit together by the joints and ligaments with which it is supplied, when each part [with power adapted to its need] is working properly [in all its functions], grows to full maturity, building itself up in love.

—Ephesians 4:16 AMPC

Jesus came in the fullness of time (Galatians 4:4). That first coming required a physical body. And I'm so glad God, for His purposes, gave Him that.

Jesus' First Coming

Jesus' death, burial, and resurrection mark the culmination of His earthly ministry and reveal the ultimate purpose of His first coming. He didn't come just to demonstrate the kingdom of God, He also came to accomplish the work of redemption through His crucifixion, burial, and resurrection. That required a body—a human body.

> That is why, when Christ came into the world, he said to God, "You did not want animal sacrifices or sin offerings. But you have given me a body to offer."
>
> —Hebrews 10:5 NLT

The epistles explore further the profound effects of Jesus' first coming in the spiritual realm. He opened the way for us to safely operate in the spirit realm and to do so as children of the living God. Jesus' work of redemption and victory over the kingdom of darkness continues to have significance for us as His ecclesia. Jesus' ministry was not limited to merely revealing the kingdom, it was also to open access for us to participate in that kingdom. And we participate as His body here in the earth. That is important!

Jesus' Second Coming—Another Body

In the same way that His first coming required His physical body, His second coming requires a body—a spiritual body that is here in the earth. What is that spiritual body?

Just as God prepared a body for Jesus' first coming, He is preparing us as His body for His second coming. He's preparing us!

Just as God prepared a body for Jesus' first coming, He is preparing us as His body for His second coming.

Now, as believers, we are invited to work alongside Him within this heavenly reality. This is where our assignment lies. We are preparing the way for the coming of the Lord, and it requires a body in much the same way that His first coming required one.

So how can you even pray into something that big? Well, the Holy Spirit helps us, but I want us to see something before we go any further.

Individualism

There was a movement in the 1700s that was first identified in the nation of France. The essence of it has been in operation since the fall of man, and we now call it "individualism." It was identified by the Greek philosopher Socrates, who emphasized self-knowledge and virtue as the foundation of a life well-lived.

Basically, individualism is the tendency in humans toward a focus on self. It's about what's important to me, what makes me happy. It's pretty much centered on "me, myself, and I."

This influence affected all of humanity in so many areas, even in the work of prayer, believe it or not! We can be so "individualistic" that we only consider our needs, our family, our challenges, our life. That's so cross-current to what God is actually interested in and how the kingdom of God operates.

God cares about the individual. Of course He does! We often find verses of scripture that mean a lot to us. So, what I have done, what you have done, and what has actually helped all of us has been to personalize the Word for us individually. Have you put your own name in it? Yes. Words in the epistles that actually refer to "we" can be made to be personal. Just insert "me." That has been a useful exercise to address a lack of ownership of the promises of God. However, in these days, the Holy Spirit is helping us to have a wider scope of vision.

Apprehended with All the Saints

The apostle Paul was chosen by the will of God to be an apostle of Jesus Christ. In his epistles to the churches, he said that he was not just writing to the pastor and leaders. He essentially wrote, "I'm writing to the whole lot of y'all. Everybody."

There's something powerful about what we get from God in a corporate assembly. The love of God is magnified when experienced with all the saints apprehending it together.

> That you may have the power and be strong to apprehend and grasp with all the saints [God's devoted people, the experience of that love] what is the breadth and length and height and depth [of it].
>
> —Ephesians 3:18 AMPC

These epistle prayers are for the Church as a whole. Though you can pray them for yourself, individually, they were meant for the body together. They become portals into the realm of the spirit. They enable you to get in the spirit to pray things for the whole body of Christ. Can we use them individually? Yes, of course. Is that how they were originally intended? No.

A Glorious Body

God is helping us to see what a glorious body this is. It's the body He is preparing for Jesus' second coming. There are many operations in this body, and we respect each one, even if it's different from our own. The leg is different from the arm. The heart is different from the liver. Each body part and organ is different from each other. But every part is needed to be a healthy body. The Holy Spirit is amplifying this in prayer. It's about waking up. The body is waking up.

Tommy Hicks had a vision back in 1961. He saw a massive giant. It was the body of Christ all over the world. And that giant began waking up and being loosed from the tethers that held it to the ground. This vision brought to our attention the working together of the body of Christ in the last days.[3]

God is helping us to see what a glorious body this is.

It doesn't have to take a long time. Many of Brother Hagin's prophecies featured the terminology "quick work." There is a work that must be done. Think about the very first prophecy of Jesus' first coming in Genesis 3:15. How many millennia did it take before Jesus finally came? It took thousands of years.

3 "Tommy Hicks Vision," *LynneHammond.org,* June 26, 2013; https://lynnehammond.org/tommy-hicks-vision/; accessed January 16, 2026.

When He finally came, after all that time of preparation, it was a quick work. He had only 30 years of His life, then only three years of intense ministry, then only three days in the grave. He died, and God raised Him up three days later. Jesus' life and work really sped up at the very end. That's what it seems to be doing right now.

The Church, the Ecclesia, has been on the earth for around 2,000 years. In all that time, we have seen wonderful ministry happening around the globe. A lovely work here and a glorious ministry there. Some are doing really well while others are doing just okay. Some parts of the body of Christ have sickly works happening. Other parts are even trying to amputate other members. It's been a bit disjointed.

Jesus is the Head of His body and as such, He knows how to get the body working as a healthy unit because He is the Savior of the body.

> ...Christ is the head of the church. He is the Savior of his body, the church.
>
> —Ephesians 5:23 NLT

Jesus is the Savior of the body. What does that mean? He can make this body glorious. And I believe in these last days, He is working this glorification of us and in us.

On the Mount of Transfiguration (Luke 9:28-36 NLT), the disciples woke up, and they saw Jesus with glory all over Him. Before the purpose of Jesus' first coming was consummated, His physical body needed to be transfigured. It was glorious. In the same way, His body in the earth today will be transfigured before the fulfilment of its purpose.

There are various things that Jesus did in His physical body that now as His body we can do. We can lay hands on the sick, and we can cast out devils. We can preach and do the work of an evangelist. It's not just because we are disciples. We are His body on the earth, and His sacrifice on the Cross made it so!

We are in union with Him. We don't just follow Him, we're in Him, and He's in us. Do you see the difference? It's a proximity that is extreme and internal. It's something far more amazing than what Peter, James, John, and the other disciples experienced on that mount.

Assistance from Heaven

There was an elderly woman I knew when I was much younger whose name was Sister Grace. Brother Hagin had a high regard for her as a prophetess. She talked about in the last days that there would be assistance from the other side—from heaven. What does that mean? Jesus had that assistance in the form of Moses and Elijah. It didn't make Him weird; it didn't make him unhinged. He got heavenly help.

We will also get help from the other side. And when we do, it won't take us long to get a lot of work done.

> No, you have come to Mount Zion, to the city of the living God, the heavenly Jerusalem, and to countless thousands of angels in a joyful gathering. You have come to the assembly of God's firstborn children, whose names are written in heaven. You have come to God himself, who is the judge over all things. You have come to the spirits of the righteous ones in heaven who have now been made perfect. You have come to Jesus, the one who mediates the new covenant between God and people, and to the sprinkled blood, which speaks of forgiveness instead of crying out for vengeance like the blood of Abel.
>
> —Hebrews 12:22-24 NLT

In Chapter 5 we saw there are many other participants in this realm. There are angels, spirits of righteous ones made perfect, Jesus, the blood—all part of this kingdom of light.

But it also says that we come to the "assembly of God's firstborn children." Well, that's not just the people on earth. Do you have anybody whose names are written in heaven—those who have gone to heaven before us? Yes! And we are joined with them. We're all in the same family. It's not uncommon to be aware of them. I certainly have been.

Now we don't take that too far and start seeking them out. Some people have done that with angels and started praying to angels and worshiping angels. And then some people started praying to saints, praying to people who were on the other side. We don't do that. We talk to the Lord. But it could be that if you are talking to our heavenly Father, and they who are in heaven are talking to our heavenly Father, we will be aware of them.

We want to be aware of His body, this body that we are part of, so we can be coordinated.

> Therefore, since we are surrounded by such a huge crowd of witnesses to the life of faith, let us strip off every weight that slows us down, especially the sin that so easily trips us up. And let us run with endurance the race God has set before us. We do this by keeping our eyes on Jesus, the champion who initiates and perfects our faith Because of the joy awaiting him, he endured the cross, disregarding its shame. Now he is seated in the place of honor beside God's throne.
>
> —Hebrews 12:1-2 NLT

The Bible clearly states that this great cloud of witnesses is cheering us on. There could be times when you're in the Spirit when you start becoming aware of our homeland too.

I believe the Church has help from heaven to start setting off the alarm and waking people up. Do you believe your prayers can go around the world and connect with people around the world? I absolutely believe it. I believe that as you pray for people here and connect with people there, you literally can fellowship in the spirit. It's the communion of saints.

United, Not Separated

One thing that the devil was hoping to get a lot of mileage out of with Covid was separation. Our separation. Separation and alienation from people. But I discovered something during that season in 2020. I didn't like to pray online, even though that seemed like our only option at the time. I would just think, *This is odd.* I couldn't get in the spirit. I had to talk to the Lord about it, and He showed me this verse.

> And the church is his body; it is made full and complete by Christ, who fills all things everywhere with himself.
>
> —Ephesians 1:23 NLT

He reminded me of the fact that there are cyber rooms, there are virtual rooms, and these are places where people gather. They gather in physical rooms, but they also gather in cyber rooms and in virtual rooms. So why couldn't we, as members of His body, pray in the same spiritual room as other believers?

There are whole communities of people who are not bound by space or time. They actually congregate and function and do business in these other kinds of rooms in the spirit. The Lord said, "Don't make it an either or." He said, "Fill everything. Fill everything. Get in every single room; get in every single thing and take up space."

When we say we want to know Him more, it will be to know the Head but also to know the body. Part of His answer is to help us to know one another. God has put people in the body as it pleased Him, and He has made us desire fellowship with one another.

We have a function together. Every joint, every connection, supplies and nourishes the body. It's not just that we like the same music or the same food. There is a function for the Church as a whole body, and we all function together in the body.

In Him We Move

I really believe the Church is positioning for some amazing movement. It isn't a twitchy movement. It isn't an uncoordinated movement. It isn't movement with one part of the body moving perfectly while it's dragging a foot along with another part of the body not moving at all.

His body was broken so that we, as His body, can become one!

Gloriously, this body, under the tutelage of the Holy Spirit, will become fluid, coordinated, and completely responsive to the Head of the Church. We are to be a body wholly flooded with light, and a body that functions in unity under the direction of the Head. His body was broken so that we, as His body, can become one!

16

COLLABORATION OF OPERATIONS

When I was praying about this movement in His presence, sometimes, sometimes as different cells are moving around, they move around one another...and then sometimes they collide into another cell, and there's an explosion of light. Have you seen any of those? It's the coolest thing. Not all of their interaction with every single cell they're close to makes that [happen], but sometimes they collide into a cell, and...it's an explosion of light. And I thought, I've had that when I bumped into some people in the spirit. ...It's not something you can manipulate. You can't calculate it. It's not something that you do with your will. It's just that when you're moving, He begins to move you around people you need to be with, and there's a divine connection...I believe those divine connections in the spirit are explosions of light.

—Patsy Cameneti, 2022

Preparation of the Body

In this preparation for the coming of the Lord, there is an urgent intensifying of the preparation of the body. I believe for this Church to be the glorious Church that we are called to be, it has to be coordinated and healthy. Spots and wrinkles are often a sign of something unhealthy internally. This body that Jesus is coming for will be without spot or wrinkle. And that will be glorious (Ephesians 5:27 AMPC).

Jesus is the Head of the Church, and all the ideas, plans, and directions for the Church in the plan of God are coming from the Head. We were not meant to go rogue, where people are on their own, going in all different directions, following what they think is the "call of God on their life." It's actually supposed to be a coordinated effort, just as the natural body needs to be coordinated in its working and action. All the action and performance is coordinated from the Head.

Collaboration

In March 2020 in a time of prayer, I received a term from the Lord, "collaboration of operations." I remember clearly the day that word came through. What I saw was that in the kingdom of God, there are different operations happening all over between different groups of people. These were in different church denominations, missions, things in the Church. Different kinds of wonderful things are happening in the Church all around the world.

There are also things happening around the world, even among those in secular and civil arenas that work as God's ministers in these arenas. In this time there is a collaboration, a coordination of those operations. They are not independent of each other, they start collaborating and working together. We could call this group of people "the good guys," who are doing great things in the earth—good things.

You know who else is simultaneously having that same working together? I saw it also happening in the kingdom of darkness. I saw different operations in the kingdom of darkness that have worked independently and have been propelled by their own wicked agendas. They didn't know of other operations or collaborations. They were busy working on their own evilness and wickedness. We could call these "the bad guys."

But now those operations are starting to collaborate, and they don't even know it. God is using even the corrupted groups of people for His

God is using even the corrupted groups of people for His purposes.

purposes. Yes, He even uses the "bad guys." We've seen in previous chapters how God has done that. For example, Caiaphas, who prophesied, or even King Herod and the Roman government who enabled the crucifixion of Jesus.

In these days, God is not only using them, they are coming together to fulfill His plan! Isn't that just amazing! Do you think that God, being sovereign, could actually use everything that He created, whether they be righteous or corrupted? Yes, indeed He can, and He does!

Used by God

There's a great promise in Isaiah 54:17 that I have used myself many times. I've said it out loud, "No weapon formed against me can prosper." But let's look at that promise in context:

> I have created the blacksmith who fans the coals beneath the forge and makes the weapons of destruction. And I have created the armies that destroy. But in that coming day no weapon turned against you will succeed. You will silence every voice raised up to accuse you. These benefits are enjoyed by the servants of the Lord; their vindication will come from me. I, the Lord, have spoken!
>
> —Isaiah 54:16-17 NLT

That's astonishing! It says that God created those who destroy! But, you say, the devil comes to steal, kill, and destroy. And he does! Well, we know that all things were created through Jesus and for Him even principalities and powers. But, as we've already seen, they are corrupt. We also know for sure that God doesn't send them to harm you. But they will come; it's not "if" but when. It's their job.

> The righteous person faces many troubles, but the Lord comes to the rescue each time.
>
> —Psalm 34:19 NLT

That's confronting *and* comforting. We know trouble comes. That's not lack of faith—that's life! Knowing how to overcome is part of the strategies God has given us. So we overcome, and we overcome on purpose!

The Good Guys and the Bad Guys

Let's look a little further. Because God originally created these principalities, it seems that God reserves the right to use them. They operate in wickedness and their corrupt agenda is to destroy, but God turns it around for His purposes. This scripture in Isaiah 54 tells us that these weapons that are formed will not harm us! Praise God, Jesus disarmed them!

> **Because God originally created these principalities, it seems that God reserves the right to use them.**

I saw how God will use the "good guys" and the "bad guys" together. No one has exclusive ownership of either good or wicked people. Remember, Peter spoke by amazing inspiration, then, just a few verses later, was being used by Satan himself.

Cogs in the Machine

All these people and groups of people will operate like cogs in a huge machine. The teeth on the cogs are details of their operations. One cog will grab on to the details of one operation, another will grab on to the details of another operation, and it turns things that have never been turned before.

In this collaboration of operations of darkness and light, high things are brought down, low things are brought up; crooked things and made straight and rough places are made smooth.

Some of those cogs in that operation turn to the left and some turn to the right. The ones that turn to the right move the ones that turn to the left. They are working in collaboration with each other. One shifts situations upward, and one shifts situations downward, but they are all working in line with the ultimate plan of God. We may only see a downward shift and may want that situation to come up, but God sees it all as part of the greater plan and is not at all concerned about downward trends because on the flipside, something is coming up.

In this collaboration of darkness and light, high things are brought down and low things are brought up; crooked things are made straight and rough places are made smooth. At the end of it all, the glory of the Lord is revealed, and all flesh shall see it together! Sound familiar?

All Working Together

All this is happening together in the kingdom of God and the kingdom of darkness. They work together, and God is working it for His plan! God is doing it, and we get to participate in our part of His majestic and mighty plan!

Things are speeding up both in the kingdom of darkness and in the kingdom of light through a coordination and collaboration of operations.

The kingdom of light and the kingdom of darkness are becoming more aware of one another. They are becoming more aware of each other's agendas. Even though they are seeming to be more at loggerheads, they are actually working together. Their collaboration may not be intentional on their part, but God is orchestrating it all. What a mighty Planner!

There is interaction between the body of Christ, the nations, and the Jews around the whole earth. The Holy Spirit in these days is making us aware, from the Head of the Church, and is lifting our attention from being only self-aware and self-absorbed, to seeing the whole picture from God's perspective.

He's getting our focus off of only what is happening with us personally or just in our family or just in our city. He's making us more aware of what's happening in the nations, in the kingdom of darkness, and in the landscape of the spiritual realm. He is unfolding to us His perfect plan from a much wider and higher perspective. What a glorious view it is from our seating with Him! This view provides us a seat where we can indeed "live peaceful and quiet lives marked by godliness and dignity" (1 Timothy 2:2 NLT).

Knowing how God is using all of His creation has really impacted the way we pray. We are no longer praying from a "skinny" place or perception of how we think God should operate. He uses everything! He is God and has the right to do that. But the most amazing thing is that He chooses to use us in that collaboration. We pray, but it's no longer according to what we think. We may have an opinion, but God blows that out of the water with His thoughts and ways; His plans are far more than we could reason by ourselves.

We don't pray, "God, help the good guys and judge the bad guys." God will use them all! That's why mercy is such a key. Mercy will cover them all and hold them until the door for mercy closes and another dispensation comes up on the horizon.

There is coming judgment on the earth, but let's cooperate with God from our seat of authority and perspective. Let's see things as God sees them and work with Him so that it is on earth as it is in heaven.

PART FIVE

WORKING IN THE KINGDOM

The ways of the kingdom are not the ways of the world. In this kingdom, we work from a place of rest. From that place of rest, there are some strategies, both spiritual and natural, that can be adopted to help you pray with others. Praying with other people in groups makes tremendous power available for the plan of God.

17

FROM REST, NOT ZEAL

> *…Once you get out of the valley and on the mountain, in the Spirit, the place of rest, you're no longer sweating bullets, time conscious and in despair. In fact, you're not seeing anything but what He shows you. Why? Because His work is all finished! You enter into rest! In this place of rest in the spirit, prayer shifts from trying to get God to do something to the delight of discovering what He has already willed!*
>
> —Patsy Cameneti, *The Spirit Realm*, 2024

He Leads Me Beside Still Waters

The 23rd Psalm is probably one of the most well-known scriptures that we use not only as sermon content, but also to bring encouragement at funerals and many other settings where calming comfort and focus on our Good Shepherd is needed and valued.

The writer of this psalm, under inspiration of the Holy Spirit, wrote the sequence of these verses with very specific purpose.

We often focus on the verses, "The Lord is my shepherd; I shall not want," and "He leads me in paths of righteousness for His name's sake." However, the verses between these two verses demonstrate something really valuable. Take a look.

> The Lord is my shepherd; I shall not want. He makes me to lie down in green pastures; He leads me beside the still waters. He

> restores my soul; He leads me in the paths of righteousness for His name's sake.
>
> —Psalm 23:1-3 NKJV

There is a purposeful insert between "The Lord is my Shepherd" and "He leads me in paths of righteousness." Before you can move in the paths He has set before you, you must lie down and rest. There is a work to be done in your soul that can only happen when you are at rest.

Before you can move in the paths He has set before you, you must lie down and rest.

This intentional rest is significant. It reminds us that even in a culture that prizes speed, efficiency, and productivity, God's character remains unchanged. He invites us to slow down, to rest in His provision, and not just consume on the run. In Middle Eastern cultures, eating is an event, a time to sit and relax. Similarly, God calls us to rest and receive, not rush ahead in our own strength, passion, or zeal.

Haste often leads us astray, especially in working with God; we may find ourselves lost in the productivity and activity of prayer, headed for the paths of righteousness, but somewhere in the middle of the prayer assignment, we'll be looking for Him and we realize that He is still waiting back at verse 2. He cannot lead you on to productivity and purpose until your soul is rested, restored, and healthy.

Jesus exemplified perfect prayer. He spent long nights in fellowship with His Father. He did not need to prop up His faith with His own thoughts and reasonings. He didn't need to get all excited and stir Himself up with His own enthusiasm or zeal. He totally rested in His Father and was at peace.

Before we are led in paths of righteousness, we must first learn to lie down in green pastures and be led beside still waters. These moments of rest and quiet listening are essential precursors to fulfilling divine assignments and receiving God's guidance.

The Still Small Voice

These moments of rest take us back to where Elijah the prophet was when he heard that "still small voice." Often God has to take us to a place where our own zeal is exhausted, our own ideas have run out of steam, and we are totally and absolutely reliant on Him. Maybe, just maybe, that is the essence of the "spirit and power of Elijah." Being still before God isn't a place of absence of everything, it is a place that gives us access to God where all distractions are removed.

Consider this. The most outstanding, heaven-and-earth-moving demonstration in Jesus' ministry happened when He was completely dead. And it was not just a type of "dead" that could be revived. He was dead and in the most inaccessible place in hell. This is where the mighty power of God alone had access to work. He needed resurrection power!

In the place where we no longer can lean to our own understanding, God is able to move. When our soul is restored to be completely aligned with Him, He is able to move us on to walking in paths of righteousness.

> For we are God's masterpiece. He has created us anew in Christ Jesus, so we can do the good things he planned for us long ago.
>
> —Ephesians 2:10 NLT

There are good works for us to do, but not the good works *we* decide on, not even the good works we may be passionate about. We are re-created in Christ Jesus to do the works *He* has planned for us.

Take No Opinion

What gives us great peace, enabling us to live a peaceful and quiet life, is when we not only trust God, but we also lay aside our own opinion. Our own opinions are based on our own assessment of any situation. Remember Peter. Jesus said that Peter was a hindrance and a trap to Him because he did not view the situation from God's perspective. Jesus recognized it was Satan that inspired Peter's comments (Matthew 16:23).

The challenge arises when we make natural assessments of situations, people, national issues, or anything that pertains to our life on earth based on our own judgment. Remember, we represent the blood of the New Covenant in Christ Jesus. His blood calls out for mercy.

Remember how the prophet Habakkuk, when faced with an impending invasion, didn't just jump to his own assessment or his own opinion of the situation. Of course, no one wants a foreign invasion and anyone could take an opinion on that situation, pleading with God to stop it! But no, he stood on his post of observation and watched to see what God would say. That, in turn, affected what Habakkuk would subsequently say.

Jesus operated in faith throughout His ministry, acting only on what He heard and saw from the Father. His greatest act, the work of redemption, was not about dynamic performances but about receiving and obeying God's directive. Jesus placed immense emphasis on receiving from the Father—the input—before any output or miracle could be performed. This principle applies to us as well; faith comes from hearing and receiving, not from our own efforts, opinions, or ideas.

Work from a Place of Rest

Do you remember what Jesus said to people who are worn out and exhausted?

> Then Jesus said, "Come to me, all of you who are weary and carry heavy burdens, and I will give you rest. Take my yoke upon you. Let me teach you, because I am humble and gentle at heart, and you will find rest for your souls."
>
> —Matthew 11:28-29 NLT

What does He give when we come to Him? He said, "I will give you rest." The Amplified Bible Classic Edition expands this to say, "I will ease, relieve, and refresh your souls." That is exactly right. True rest is the soul being refreshed in His presence. There is nothing like the peace and renewal that comes from being with Him.

We Get to Work

In that verse Jesus goes on to say, "Take my yoke upon you." What? I thought we were going to rest, but taking a yoke speaks of work! Yes, that's what they put on beasts of burden before they send them out to work, and work hard!

That yoke does speak of work! Jesus didn't say "Learn from me because I am mighty and strong!" No, He said, *"Let me teach you, because I am humble and gentle at heart, and you will find rest for your souls"* (Matthew 11:29 NLT).

Herein lies the secret. It's about being humble under the mighty hand of God that will enable you to work from a place of rest.

There is a labor we must do first before we do any work in the kingdom of God. It's laboring to enter rest. Then, from that place of rest, we can work, not in our own strength but yoked to Him and drawing from His strength.

There is much kingdom work to be done! But the work of the kingdom will never be accomplished through human effort and passionate zeal. As scripture says, "Not by might, nor by power, but by My Spirit" (Zechariah 4:6 NKJV). This isn't just a phrase we quote. It's a spiritual reality. God's purposes are not fulfilled through human zeal, emotion, or determination, though there are certainly moments when we pray boldly and act courageously. Our strength, however, is not the source; the Holy Spirit empowers us for God's work.

The work of the kingdom will never be accomplished through human effort and passionate zeal.

Those who have entered into His rest have stopped striving in their own strength. The same applies to prayer. People of faith must learn to cease from frantic, desperate praying, assuming they will be heard because of the volume or intensity or even passion of their words.

The truest and most effective prayers are not born from our own ideas or urgency. They come from God. He already knows the work He intends to accomplish, so He supplies the prayer that brings it forth. Our role is to yield, listen, and partner with Him, trusting His Spirit to lead, empower, and complete the work.

It's for us to do what is necessary to "come unto Him" and actually get into the spirit where His will and His works are already established! A real place of *rest*. It exists. In that place you start being aware of God's great purposes and can begin cooperating with those amazing purposes. From that place you will find rest for your soul, not working from the strength of your soul but from His strength. God's works!

Following Divine Directives

In special military operations, those entrusted with the most critical missions are not chosen for their marksmanship or skill alone but for their strict obedience and ability to follow orders. During the aftermath of 9/11, the whole nation was impassioned, and everyone wanted to go, bring their own gun and fix the problem. They wanted to do something!

During that time, I heard a special operations soldier being interviewed. The interviewer asked him what he would do if he came upon Osama Bin Laden. I could hear it in the interviewer's voice. She, like many others, was impassioned. But the special ops soldier simply replied, "I would complete my objective." She asked again, rephrasing the question in an attempt to elicit a more passionate response. He gave the same reply with the same tone of voice, "I would complete my objective." His unwavering focus on the mission, rather than emotional response or dramatic action, was precisely why he was trusted with such critical assignments.

Similarly in our walk with God, we do not receive assignments because of our talents, zeal, or even our passion—but because we can follow His directives faithfully, accurately, and completely.

Jesus demonstrated this kind of obedience in His ministry. Despite being surrounded by need, He remained focused on His mission: "I am sent only to the lost house of Israel." Even when others, like the Syrophoenician woman or the centurion, reached into His assignment by faith and received miracles, Jesus maintained clarity about His directive. His perfection lay in His unwavering obedience to the Father, directed only by the Holy Spirit. Of course, their faith reached into a dispensation that was to come, and they received healing by faith.

Like soldiers who act only when given a directive, we must wait, listen, and respond to God's voice. Acting without a divine directive leads to confusion and misstep.

This kind of prayer, acting under the direction of God, is what characterized that part of Elijah's mission. Remember, his passion and zeal for the Lord turned out not to be the most effective way that God removed the worshippers of Baal. It was after a period of quiet and listening to the "still small voice" that Elijah received those three directives from God. God was able to do far more with Elijah's obedience than Elijah did running on his own zeal.

Restore and Cleanse Your Soul

The output of Jesus' ministry is seen in the miracles and the healings and everything He did. Jesus couldn't have done any of it at all without input from His Father. Could it be any different for us? It cannot because that's how faith comes. It comes by every word that comes from the Father's mouth.

Lying down in green pastures and beside still waters is of primary importance. Having our souls restored is key, so that there isn't a mixture of bits of us with the pure water that comes from the throne of God.

When our soul is restored, healed, and in unity with our spirit, we don't put bits of ourselves in and muddy the pure water that flows through us from the throne of God. You are a vessel of His and dispense His word, His life, His power, and wisdom.

If you were to eat at a restaurant and there was something stuck on your plate other than the food you ordered, you wouldn't care how good the food was, you'd want another meal that was served on a plate that wasn't contaminated.

Sometimes we may be dispensing waters of life in prayer through vessels that have clumps of aggravation, frustration, or your own opinion like contaminated vessels. Just as we would reject dirty utensils, we must let God's living water cleanse us from aggravation, frustration, and hardened opinions.

The living water of the Holy Spirit purges us, allowing us to pray and minister without the contamination of personal bias. As we let that cleansing, living water flow through us, our hardened opinions soften, and we become open vessels, ready to receive and dispense life-giving water.

Why not take a moment to drink deeply from the Holy Spirit, allowing His pure and clean water to restore, cleanse, and refresh our souls.

18

PRAYER GROUP PRACTICALITIES

Believers who have learned how to work together with God in the spirit have the privilege and pleasure of also helping to bring God's purposes to pass on the earth through prayer. Through prophetic or Spirit-led prayer, they actually become a conduit of God's purposes being fulfilled on the earth. This is not because the prayers are prayed by prophets but because the prayer content is inspired by God....

—Patsy Cameneti, *The Spirit Realm*, 2024

Let's Pray

It's wonderful to know so much about prayer. The ways and purposes of God are intriguing. It's a deeply satisfying endeavor to work with God in the realm of the spirit. It's fascinating to discover the spiritual landscape in which we function. And it's amazing to realize just how powerful prayer really is and how important it is in unfolding the plan of God in the earth. Armed with all this knowledge, what do we do now?

What we do is we pray! And we can pray in unity with other believers. There is tremendous power in united prayer. Jesus gave the quorum size for a prayer group. He said, "Where two or three are gathered together in My name, I am there in the midst of them" (Matthew 18:20 NKJV).

It's a deeply satisfying endeavor to work with God in the realm of the spirit.

You only need two or three participants to make a prayer group. More is better, but two or three is enough. I have found that some of our most effective groups have only three or four people.

Don't be afraid to start a prayer group. If you invite the Holy Spirit and acknowledge your need of Him to pray, He will accommodate your willingness, and He will be right there to help you. Listen to Him. He will lead you well.

Leading a Prayer Group

As a leader of a prayer group, you have a holy assignment as you help gather people to pray. You're participating in making things on earth as they are in heaven!

The following are a few practical ways to help you do that. Please feel free to use these in your church prayer groups as you deem them helpful.

You are functioning within the operation of your local church and are a vital part of the ministry's operation. Never bring what's been prayed out of the prayer room to instruct or direct your pastor or leadership. If God is able to trust you to keep things in the place of prayer, you will find He will give you more to pray and more insight in the Spirit.

Tremendous Power Is Made Available

As you work together with one heart and one voice, the power of God is made available. You have no need to require a "feeling" or "goosebumps." Simply know that when you meet to pray in His name, He is there in the midst, and power is being made available.

> ...The earnest (heartfelt, continued) prayer of a righteous man makes tremendous power available [dynamic in its working].
> —James 5:16 AMPC

This power of prayer is necessary for building the body of Christ. As you pray, the Holy Spirit will adapt the power according to the need. You are not responsible for who takes up that power. You simply make it available because there is a power-draw from the body of Christ or whomever is in need of that power.

> For because of Him the whole body (the church, in all its various parts), closely joined and firmly knit together by the joints and ligaments with which it is supplied, when each part [with power adapted to its need] is working properly [in all its functions], grows to full maturity, building itself up in love.
> —Ephesians 4:16 AMPC

Prayer Always Starts with God

The best way to get your prayer assignments is to seek God for them. Sometimes provocation to pray will happen from external sources, but when you take those situations to God, He will direct your prayer. Prayer is not about what's on your heart as much as it is about what is on God's heart. Ask Him, "What's on your heart today, Lord?"

Romans 8:26 clearly states that we don't know how to pray effectively, but the Holy Spirit comes to our aid to help.

Prayer lists or our own ideas are not the place to start, even if this way of praying has seemed to be effective in the past. Your own zeal can appear to have some short-term effects, but as we have seen with the example of Elijah, the most effective and long-reaching prayer is when we pray by the unction and direction of God Himself.

In our church, we have a number of prayer groups that focus on particular issues. For example, there may be a group that prays for youth or for families or for Israel. But even these focus topics are directed by

God, and what is prayed in these groups from week to week is also directed by God.

We listen to what God has to say about any and every situation. He will confirm what you hear from His Word.

Habakkuk's Example

We see in Habakkuk's example three easy steps to take when starting to pray.

First, Habakkuk set himself in his watching place. You can do that by simply acknowledging what Jesus has done to give you seating with Him in heavenly places. Worship Him for it; thank Him for what He's done, and acknowledge your seating with Jesus in heavenly places.

Second, stop to listen or to see with your heart. You can wait in silent anticipation, or you can pray in the spirit, but He will always give you a prompting in your heart as to what He wants to say or the direction He wants you to go.

Third, say what you see or what you hear. It may be something you see, then describe it to Him. It may be something you hear, then speak it out. Or it may be a portion of scripture, then read it. When all of this is directed to God, He will add more to it (Habakkuk 2:1; Jeremiah 1:11-12 NKJV).

This is not by any means a rigid formula, but it is a common trend that has been helpful as a starting point in the prayer groups in our church. The Holy Spirit may lead you in different ways, but as you learn to flow together, this will be a helpful way to start.

Pray in Spirit and in Truth

When Jesus spoke to the woman at the well, He gave her a powerful spiritual principle related to worship. This same principle applies any time we engage with God, especially in prayer.

> God is a Spirit (a spiritual Being) and those who worship Him must worship Him in ***spirit*** and in ***truth*** (reality).
>
> —John 4:24 AMPC

So, there are two important elements in our prayer: in spirit and in truth.

In the Spirit

Praying in the Spirit is following the Holy Spirit as He guides our prayer. This also includes praying in tongues, which is probably the best way to get in the spirit initially. You can also sing and worship Him. That's a wonderful way to get in the spirit. Using every access point that has been given by and through Jesus will help you to get in the spirit.

Being "in the spirit" is simply being more aware of God and the realm of the spirit than of the natural realm, or the things that impact our natural senses.

In Truth

One of the most effective tools we have for prayer is the Word of God, the Bible. When we use the Word of God and allow the Holy Spirit to wield this supernatural sword, we can pray most effectively.

We've used the Word of God in our prayer groups in tandem with anything the Holy Spirit shows us in prayer. We will often say, "Lord, show that to us in the Word." Then He will give a scripture to back up what it is He is showing us.

A New Testament Pattern

Throughout the book of Acts, a New Testament pattern for corporate prayer emerges. When the believers prayed in unity, the operations of the Holy Spirit were manifested. Every believer can join with other believers and be a vessel for the Holy Spirit to use in the operation of prayer.

> Once when he was eating with them, he commanded them, "Do not leave Jerusalem until the Father sends you the gift he promised, as I told you before."
>
> —Acts 1:4 NLT

> They all met together and were constantly united in prayer....
>
> —Acts 1:14 NLT

Is a Group Leader Needed?

While we are committed to following the leading of the Holy Spirit in prayer, there needs to be someone who can lead the group as they follow the Holy Spirit. The leadership principle is seen often throughout the New Testament.

Believers are instructed to enlist under the leader.

> I urge you to pay all deference to such leaders and to enlist under them and be subject to them, as well as to everyone who joins and cooperates [with you] and labors earnestly.
>
> —1 Corinthians 16:16 AMPC

Different Flows and Styles

There are many different flows or styles of prayer, just as there are many different types of prayer. Each person will bring their own unique style to the group. As a leader, it's important that you value every style and help everyone to not only identify their style but learn to flow with it.

Some pray-ers will be quiet and not say much. Some will "see" things or "hear" things in their hearts. Some will get words of scripture to read. Learning to work together as a united prayer group can take time.

There are some practical things you can do to help everyone be in unity, but the most important is that they are all listening to the Holy Spirit. This kind of prayer is Spirit-led and Spirit-fed.

It's also important to remember that just as there are many different styles of prayer, there are many different styles of leading in prayer.

Identify how you lead as a prayer leader, and flow in that style confidently and under the direction of the Holy Spirit.

What You Do as the Leader

PREPARATION

- Pray about your prayer group.
- Clearly identify the general focus and purpose of your prayer group.
- Ask God for the scriptural foundation for your prayer group and for your general focus. It becomes an anchor and launch place every time you meet to pray.
- Pray for your prayer group members.

SPIRITUAL

- Encourage the pray-ers to bring their supply, and pray for them.

> Well, my brothers and sisters, let's summarize. When you meet together, one will sing, another will teach, another will tell some special revelation God has given, one will speak in tongues, and another will interpret what is said. But everything that is done must strengthen all of you.
>
> —1 Corinthians 14:26 NLT

Sometimes it's helpful to draw out of a group member what they may be "seeing" or "hearing." Ask someone, "What are you seeing?" They may say, "I don't know." Then ask, "What do you think you see?" Never dismiss what they say. Everyone is on a learning path.

Remember, you've come to pray to God. It's okay to spend a few minutes fellowshipping with each other, but when it's time to pray, *pray!*

Talk to God as you pray, not to each other.

PRACTICAL

Determine how best to lead the group. Initially you may need to take a strong lead by doing most of the praying yourself, leading the group, and just having them follow on in agreement with you. As the group learns and becomes more familiar with the direction of the Holy Spirit, you may give the lead to someone else for a little bit then take it back again. Pretty soon, your group will be able to identify the leading of the Holy Spirit in their midst, and they will transfer from looking to you to lead to looking to the Holy Spirit. It's amazing and so thrilling to all be together in unity, being led by the Holy Spirit. He is a good Leader!

Assign a person to take notes. Written notes not only help you keep a track of what the Spirit of God is saying, but it documents the Word of God.

Be on the lookout for potential prayer leaders who could lead their own group. Start by assigning them to lead your group from time to time. It may be helpful for you as the leader to take a day off and let them lead without you being there.

Prayer Group Etiquette

Praying in a prayer group is different from praying alone. Here are some suggestions that will help you all work together.

- Learn to identify the flow of the group and follow the leader in that flow.
- Follow the leader and the focus that has been set. Don't switch the topic until the leader switches it.
- With one ear, listen to the Holy Spirit; with the other ear, listen to the members of the prayer group.
- Don't pray so loudly that the other group members cannot hear the leader or each other.
- Don't do anything to draw attention to yourself or distract the others who are praying.
- When someone prays something in English, stop what you are praying and engage your heart with that prayer. Look in your heart for agreement.

- Keep your mind quiet and your heart engaged, constantly aware of the presence of God and the leading of the Holy Spirit.
- If it seems like the unction has lifted, don't assume you're finished. Keep praying in tongues, and hold your place in your heart. However, when the prayer is finished, then finish!

Prayer Meeting Flow

- Start with the Word of God. Bring a short scripture and encouragement to prayer.
- Spend a little time in worship and acknowledgment of God.
- Set the focus, and open the prayer time with prayer.
- Pray! Keep your focus on talking to God, not each other.
- Try not to break the flow to explain or share with the group. You can do that at the end. Occasionally, it is helpful to interpret what is happening and the flow of the Holy Spirit. This is helpful if the group is still learning.
- You may need to keep your group members on track and encourage them to "say it to God" rather than talking to each other.
- When the prayer time is finished, the group can then share with each other. Times of sharing are really valuable!

Debrief and Discussion

- When the prayer time is over, don't forget to worship and give thanks to God.
- Acknowledge the help of the Holy Spirit and the access that Jesus has obtained for you to work with God in the Spirit realm.
- Now would be the time you can open the discussion on what the group has seen or heard in the spirit.
- This is a good opportunity to identify and collate what the Spirit of God has been saying.

- Remember this. What's said in the prayer group stays in the prayer group. What you do with what you've seen and heard is important. Keep it in the prayer room.

Talking to One Another

I have found that there are times we will talk to one another in a prayer group and spend a little less time in prayer and more time talking. While it seems to contradict what's just been suggested, these times of talking can be really valuable. When we talk to one another, we are not simply discussing the events of the day or the situations in the world. We are engaging in conversation where God is in the midst. We talk and unpack things of God, insights, the Word, and the ways of God. These times can be holy and very much "in the Spirit."

> Then those who feared the Lord talked often one to another; and the Lord listened and heard it, and a book of remembrance was written before Him of those who reverenced and worshipfully feared the Lord and who thought on His name.
>
> —Malachi 3:16 AMPC

God Needs Us

God has a Great Master Plan, and He knows every detail of that plan. He needs our voice to enable His power to work out this plan on earth. He prepared a body for Jesus when He came the first time; He is preparing a body for Himself as we prepare for Jesus' return. We are His body in the earth. He needs us to pray by His unction in order to bring heaven's master plan to earth.

He needs us to pray by His unction to bring heaven's master plan to earth.

Even so, come Lord Jesus!

EPILOGUE

by Jenny Eddison

This book is full of practical strategies and information about prayer, particularly for the end times. And, as we've already mentioned, this was born out of many years of working together with God in prayer.

Now armed with all this information, and revelation, we could mistakenly assume that preparing for the Lord's return relies almost exclusively on us declaring His will on earth. However, God's plans are already written in heaven, and He will do what He has planned. We have no authority to act on our own understanding, but the Holy Spirit guides our prayers. Much remains to be revealed and unfolded both in heaven and on earth.

God's part is bigger. We simply cooperate with Him.

There is a key for the unfolding of His plans—one that can often be overlooked.

In the book of Revelation, the first three chapters deal with the Church—exposure, exhortation, and even warnings. Then in chapters 4 and 5 we see a shift in focus to the heavenlies and what is being opened for the days that follow—the last days.

Revelation 5:1-5 (NLT):

> Then I saw a scroll in the right hand of the one who was sitting on the throne. There was writing on the inside and the outside of the scroll, and it was sealed with seven seals. And I saw a strong angel, who shouted with a loud voice: "Who is worthy to break the seals on this scroll and open it?" But no one in heaven or on earth or under the earth was able to open the scroll and read it.

> Then I began to weep bitterly because no one was found worthy to open the scroll and read it. But one of the twenty-four elders said to me, "Stop weeping! Look, the Lion of the tribe of Judah, the heir to David's throne has won the victory. He is worthy to open the scroll and its seven seals."

There are many scrolls to be opened in these days—plans, events, collaborations of operations, but there is only One who is worthy to open those scrolls—the Lord Jesus Christ alone!

What triggers these opening? It's worship!

Revelation 5:9-14 (NKJV):

> And they sang a new song, saying:
> "You are worthy to take the scroll,
> And to open its seals;
> For You were slain,
> And have redeemed us to God by Your blood
> Out of every tribe and tongue and people and nation,
> And have made us kings and priests to our God;
> And we shall reign on the earth."
>
> Then I looked, and I heard the voice of many angels around the throne, the living creatures, and the elders; and the number of them was ten thousand times ten thousand, and thousands of thousands, saying with a loud voice:
> "Worthy is the Lamb who was slain
> To receive power and riches and wisdom,
> And strength and honor and glory and blessing!"
>
> And every creature which is in heaven and on the earth and under the earth and such as are in the sea, and all that are in them, I heard saying:
> "Blessing and honor and glory and power
> Be to Him who sits on the throne,
> And to the Lamb, forever and ever!"

Then the four living creatures said, "Amen!"
And the twenty-four elders fell down and worshiped Him who lives forever and ever.

Jesus is the Alpha and Omega. By Him all things were created and hold together. He alone is worthy to open the scrolls, and they will be opened for us to see and to work with. But the key is worship!

Worship Him today and watch to see what He will unfold for you. That sets you up to be able to collaborate with Him as we watch and wait for His return!

The following is a song Patsy and I would often sing:

He's coming soon, He's coming soon.
With joy we welcome His returning.
It may be morn, it may be night or noon,
I know, I know He's coming soon.

—Thoro Harris, 1917–1944

PROPHECY

Patsy Cameneti
January 16, 2025

I see a calendar. I see a calendar, and there is a deadline for some things to be done. A deadline for some things to be done.

Up to this time, it's been on time, but if it goes at this rate, it will not be on time. There is an acceleration to the work, and so there's going to be a supply of the Spirit that enables a quickening and people joining together with great skill to be able to do and ideas to know how to pick up the pace, Hallelujah!

It becomes so apparent to you to be able to do what He's called you to do…. Dreams, visions, people sent to those nations…people coming from the nations that He assigned you to, oh! For He is, He is causing the networks of the nations to become very identifiable and tangible in your spirit….

And churches connected not just to themselves and connected not just to those of friends, of people close by…but we are connected across the body…and you're going to wake up hearing the cries of those in the body of Christ in another nation, and you will assist them…and there's going to be even, even divine (this is odd) divine travel to those places… to assist, to assist, to assist….

For nothing more will happen until you follow after love…but dramatic gifts of the spirit will be on display as you follow after love… embrace, embrace, embrace what He has given to you right now.

He's given it.

He has given it to you!

ABOUT PATSY CAMENETI AND JENNY EDDISON

Patsy Cameneti

Patsy has lived and ministered in diverse cultures and social settings around the world. She had a unique ability to simplify complicated spiritual truths and impart these to believers of many diverse cultures and backgrounds.

Her life inspired others to live out of an authentic relationship with God, and her voice continues to be an influence in the body of Christ, even though she has now taken up residence in heaven.

Patsy, along with her husband Tony, served as senior pastors of Rhema Family Church and directors of Rhema Bible Training College in Australia and Papua New Guinea. Tony continues to serve in these roles.

Jenny Eddison

Jenny worked closely with Patsy since the Camenetis first arrived in Australia. She served as both her ministry assistant and prayer partner. Jenny leads the Prayer Ministry at Rhema Family Church Brisbane where she and her husband, James, serve as associate pastors.

With a background in education, Jenny has the ability to break down spiritual concepts and help believers apply these concepts to practical settings. She has a strong desire to help train and equip believers to work with God in prayer.

Jenny and James are also instructors at Rhema Bible Training College Australia and Papua New Guinea.